Believe
in Love

Believe
in Love

THE LIFE, MINISTRY AND TEACHINGS
OF JOHN PAUL II

BRENDAN LEAHY

New City Press
Hyde Park, New York

Published in the United States by New City Press
202 Comforter Blvd., Hyde Park, NY 12538
www.newcitypress.com
©2011 Brendan Leahy

First published 2011 by Veritas Publications
7/8 Lower Abbey Street
Dublin 1 Ireland
Email publications@veritas.ie
Website www.veritas.ie

Cover design by Tanya M. Ross

A copy of the CIP data is available from the Library of Congress.

ISBN 978-1-56548-421-4

Printed in the United States of America

Acknowledgements

This book has been put together in a short period of time and I wish to acknowledge with gratitude the contribution of all friends and colleagues in the Focolare Movement and in St Patrick's College, Maynooth who offered me useful advice, help and encouragement. In particular I am grateful to Maura Hyland, Donna Doherty and Julie Steenson of Veritas as well as Julie James and Gary Brandl of New City Press. Unless otherwise indicated, the texts from Vatican and Papal documents quoted throughout the book are taken from the Vatican website (www.vatican.va).

Contents

Preface

So many people came into contact with Pope John Paul in one way or another that there's probably an almost endless number of stories to be shared. Mine would be of the morning of 13 May 1991 when, together with about forty others, I attended the Pope's early-morning Mass. Later that day he was due to go to Fatima, ten years after the assassination attempt on his life. After Mass, he greeted each one of us personally, without any trace of being in a rush. He even stopped, when requested, for a group photograph. Jokingly, he concluded our time together, saying, 'And now it's time for breakfast!'

I turned on the television that evening and saw him in Fatima with one million pilgrims. The thought occurred to me that whether it was saying Mass, greeting us that morning, going for breakfast, or being with a million pilgrims, what mattered for John Paul II was to live the present moment well – each moment directed towards God in his will and towards the neighbour in love. Each person was important to him. In every trip he made he wanted to make personal contact and people felt that deeply.

John Paul was a man who let himself be shaped by the two great commandments: love of God with all your heart, soul and mind, and love of your neighbour as yourself. Then God did his part: 'The Almighty God has done great things for me.' So many wonderful things happened around Pope John Paul through his life, ministry and teaching.

This short work offers a guided journey through many aspects of that life, ministry and teaching. I have gathered the material into sections that readily suggested themselves – his life before becoming Pope; the main foundations of his teaching; his spirituality; his vision of the Church and then sections on John Paul as pastor, man of dialogue and builder of the civilisation of love. Within each section there are short chapters on various topics. While all the sections and chapters are interrelated, each chapter can be taken on its own for reflection or used for study purposes. I've provided references for those who want to pursue further their exploration of any of the topics dealt with. Above all, I hope the book will be enjoyable to read and of benefit to you, the reader.

Towards the end of his life, John Paul repeated something he had said on many other occasions: 'the sense of being an "unworthy servant" is growing in me in the midst of all that happens around me – and I think I feel at ease with this'.[1] It was perhaps yet another way of saying something he had lived throughout his life – in all circumstances believe in love. Prompted by the Spirit, he wanted to make that merciful love of God known. In his beatification by Pope Benedict, the 'unworthy servant' Pope John Paul continues to be a beacon of light showing us the way: believe in love, always.

Brendan Leahy
St Patrick's College
Maynooth

On the Way to
Becoming Pope

'*Deo Gratias!* My deepest gratitude for the gift of a vocation.'

~ *Gift and Mystery*

The Early Years
'The war radically changed the course of my life'

When you are young, you have dreams, hopes and expectations. Karol Jósef Wojtyła, born in 1920 in Wadowice in Poland, was no different. His father was an army captain and his mother, Emilia, occasionally took on sewing to help supplement the family's income. The year of Wojtyła's birth was an auspicious one, the same in which a free Poland emerged out of the Treaty of Versailles. He was the third and last child (a sister, Olga, had died in infancy). 'Lolek' – as he was affectionately called – grew up well, studying, playing football and going on summer holidays with friends, many of whom were Jews. Wintertime was for ice-skating. Later, he would take up canoeing and mountaineering.

Suffering, however, touched Wojtyła's life at an early age. His forty-five-year-old mother's death, when he was not yet even nine years old, was a hard blow. So too was his brother Edmund's death from scarlet fever, when Wojtyła was about twelve. And yet life moves on. His father, Karol senior, began looking after the house, preparing both breakfast and an evening meal, while at lunchtime the two would go to a small eating house nearby. His father, himself a profoundly spiritual man, brought his son on visits to shrines such as Kalwaria. In 1931, they went to the famous Jasna Góra shrine of the Black Madonna at Czestochowa.

At second-level school, the future Pope developed a passion for theatre. Sometimes he was a producer of plays, other times an actor, often performing with Halina Krolikiewiczowna. He later recalled:

> Certainly, I knew many girls from school and, involved as I was in the school drama club, I had many opportunities to get together with other young people. But this was not the issue. At that time I was completely absorbed by a passion for literature, especially dramatic literature, and for the theatre.[2]

When he had finished school, Wojtyła moved to Kraków with his father, where he enrolled in the famous Jagiellonian University in 1938. All was in place for him to pursue his passion for studying the Polish language and literature.

But then everything crumbled. On a Friday morning, 1 September 1939, when he went to the Wawel Cathedral, he found it empty. The German aeroplanes had begun to fly overhead. Soon the bombardment began. Hitler's invasion of Poland was to take Wojtyła away from his studies. The university was shut down and the lecturers were deported to the Sachsenhausen concentration camp. Queuing for food was now the order of the day. All of this, as he put it, 'radically changed the course of my life' (8).

The war was also the period when Wojtyła lost his father, who died of a heart attack. He remarked that because of its suddenness, his father's death affected him even more than his mother's had, not least because he wasn't there when he died. All his earlier plans, the study of the Polish language and letters, began to fade: 'In a way it was like being uprooted from the soil in which, up till that moment, my humanity had grown' (34).

In order to avoid deportation and forced labour, in the autumn of 1940 he began to work in the stone quarry attached to the Solvay chemical plant. Here too he came face to face with the fragility of life. During the detonation of dynamite, some rocks struck a worker and killed him – the sight of the dead young man left a deep impression on the young Wojtyła.

Life was anything but secure for him: he could have been arrested any day – at home or in the stone quarry – and taken away to a concentration camp. His friends became very important. As did his involvement in the clandestine theatrical world, playing to small audiences of some twenty people in private flats. And yet Wojtyła was searching for something more in his life.

He read intensely and soon it began to dawn on him that the theatre was not his vocation. Helped by friends and colleagues, he began to see there was another away. An 'interior illumination' gradually persuaded him that God had a plan – as if he was saying to him: 'Give yourself totally to me.' Soon it became clear that this meant 'the Lord wants me to become a priest' (35). With this awareness came joy, peace and ardour. In the autumn of 1942, while he continued working and living in lodgings with a family, Wojtyła entered the 'unusual seminary' operating under the future Cardinal Sapieha, who was then Archbishop (13).

None of us can be sure of what's ahead of us, so it is best to live the present moment well. Wojtyła was to discover this many times in his life.

On 29 February 1944, coming home from a double shift at the plant, he was knocked down by a lorry of Nazi soldiers. He lost consciousness. A woman, Jozefa Florek, who was passing by on a tram at that very moment, saw what happened, hopped off the tram and ran towards him. In another act of the hand of providence, the German officer in command happened to pass by in his car. Seeing the situation, he ordered Jozefa to bring water and wipe away the blood. He then ordered a transport lorry to bring Wojtyła to hospital, where he remained in a coma for around nine hours. He was to remain in hospital for two weeks. No lasting damage was done, but it could have been a fateful day.

By now the war was raging intensely. On 1 August 1944, Warsaw rose up against the Germans. In reaction, eighty thousand people were arrested in Kraków. The German soldiers burst into the house where Wojtyła was lodging, opening many rooms but not the room where he was kneeling in prayer. The situation was clearly precarious so Cardinal Sapieha came to the decision that it was safer for the seminarians to go and live in the bishop's house. The time had come, therefore, for Wojtyła to leave the Solvay plant.

Eventually, on the night of 17 January 1945, the Germans abandoned Kraków and the following morning the Soviet troops moved in. Poland was liberated from the Nazi nightmare but, although it was not immediately apparent, a cold new era was about to begin. For Wojtyła the time for ordination had come, and on 1 November 1946 – All Saints Day – he was ordained priest.

Looking back years later at all these events, he was able to say, 'Certainly, in God's plan nothing happens by chance' (34).

Doctoral Studies, 1946–1948
'In Rome time vanishes ... doing God's will'

Karol Wojtyła was ordained earlier than the rest of his class because his archbishop had decided he should go to Rome to finish his studies. In less than a month after his ordination he was on his way. It was a time of great excitement for the young man. It was his first time abroad, and as he passed through Prague, Nuremberg, Strasbourg and Paris, little could he have imagined how many journeys he would undertake in his life. He recalls visiting the Polish Seminary, formerly the Irish College, at rue des Irlandais in Paris where they stayed 'only briefly, since time was pressing'.[3]

Reaching Rome in the last days of November, he enrolled in a two-year doctoral programme at the Dominican Angelicum University. He had been given good advice by Father Karol Kozłowski, rector of the Kraków seminary, who told him that it was more important to get to know Rome itself than to simply study. He took that advice, getting to know not just the city of Peter and Paul with its monuments and history, its catacombs, martyrs and confessors, but also the innovative forms of apostolate then developing in the Church and spoken of in Rome. He began to understand the mutual correlation existing between priestly service and apostolate of the laity.

It was during these two years that he visited Belgium, France and Holland. He became aware of the significant impact on the Church of cultural developments in Western Europe. For instance, Henri Godin and Yvan Daniel had just published the book *La France, Pays de Mission?* (*France, a Country of Mission?*), causing quite a stir. The 'elder daughter of the Church' had become mission territory! He began to appreciate more deeply that 'the Europe of the post-war period, a Europe of splendid Gothic cathedrals' was 'a Europe threatened by increasing secularization'. He could see there was a 'need to confront this impending danger through new forms of pastoral activity open to a broader participation by the laity' (56).

New active organisations and lively ecclesial communities then emerging in the Church appealed to him. Living at the Belgian College in Rome he became aware, for instance, of worker-priests and the Young Christian Worker movement. His stay in Rome was clearly providing 'a more profound vision of the Church' (59).

The period of 1946–1948 was of course primarily one of study for Wojtyła, and lead to the defence of his thesis research on 19 June 1948. His topic was 'The Doctrine of Faith in St John of the Cross'.[4] Why did he choose to study the sixteenth-century mystic-theologian? One reason was the influence of a layman mentor back in Kraków, Jan Tyranowski, who had introduced the young Wojtyła to the writings of both John of the Cross and Teresa of Avila. His thesis moderator was Father Garrigou-Lagrange – the famous spiritual theologian whose writings are still quoted today – and attending his lessons was probably another major factor in his choice of topic, as Garrigou-Lagrange too had written on John of the Cross. Furthermore, the fourth centenary of the saint's death had just been celebrated in 1942 and Edith Stein had dedicated a full work to him entitled *The Science of the Cross*. Perhaps the Spanish theologian, philosopher, mystic, poet and spiritual man simply appealed to the young Polish priest because of his own poetic-spiritual passion.

Wojtyła had his work cut out for him; he had to deal with historical, textual and doctrinal questions regarding John of the Cross. But to this task he brought his education and the languages he had by now picked up – Italian, French, German and Spanish – making sure to always refer to the original text in the Castilian language.

In John of the Cross's works, starting with *Ascent to Mount Carmel*, it is clear that the basis of the Christian life lies in faith, hope and charity. This is the heart of his asceticism-mysticism, the centre of his graced anthropology that Wojtyła admired. Our faith journey is a progressive dynamic of active and passive purification of the senses and of the spirit, leading us to perfect union with God. The virtue of faith needs to be informed by hope and charity to reach full union with God, the union to which it is disposed by its nature under the action of the Holy Spirit.

Garrigou-Lagrange had a maxim that ran: 'The perfection of theology does not consist in the deduction of a new conclusion but in the deeper penetration of its principles.'[5] Wojtyła's thesis reflects this. It is indeed a deep, sapiential consideration of the theme of faith in John of the Cross's writings, examining his Christocentrism and concluding that there is both a concordance with, as well as some differences between, the doctrine of John of the Cross and that of Thomas Aquinas.

Karol Wojtyła had gained much from his time in Rome, which had flown by. As he wrote to a Polish friend, Helena Szkocka: 'my time vanishes with enormous speed ... I really don't know how a year and a half has gone by. Study, observation, meditation ... Each day is tightly filled. It gives me the sense that I am serving God according to my possibilities and according to his will.'[6]

Student, Pastor and University Lecturer
*'Studying theology and philosophy but not forgetting
I was a priest'*

Back in Poland in 1948, Wojtyła was appointed to the very poor rural
parish of Niegowici, thirty miles east of Kraków. Some even considered
this to be a dead end in his priestly career, but the enthusiastic young
priest – on the back of his academic success – plunged himself into
pastoral work: teaching, celebrating Mass, hearing confessions, visiting
families, blessing homes, calling on the sick, marrying couples and
christening babies. He was careful to build up the community, and
together with another priest he promoted within the parish the same
Living Rosary Movement he had been a member of as a young man. He
also organised a drama circle and produced plays.

Soon he was appointed to St Florian's Church in Kraków. This was
a city parish attended by a lot of young university students and brought
him into contact with many intellectuals and artists. Every Thursday
he organised open conferences to discuss issues, and so a 'Wojtyła
circle' came into being. During this time he resumed composing poetry,
worked on a new drama and took private English lessons. In 1949, he
began writing articles for the Catholic newspaper *Tygodnik Powszechny*
and would continue to do so for the next thirty years, building up a great
friendship with editor Jerzy Turowicz.

In November 1951, Wojtyła was sent by Archbishop Baziak to
pursue studies for another doctorate that would qualify him to become
an assistant university professor. The thesis topic he chose was not
an easy one: 'An Assessment of the Possibility of Erecting a Christian
Ethic on the Principles of Max Scheler'. The German phenomenologist,
Max Scheler, of mixed Jewish and Protestant heritage, had converted to
Catholicism and was a follower of Edmund Husserl, who is regarded as
the father of phenomenology. One of Husserl's close collaborators was
Edith Stein who had been put to death during the war – as Pope, John
Paul II would beatify her and later name her patron of Europe.

The phenomenologist approach to philosophy proposes that we
only gradually grasp the truth concerning a particular question through

extensive rumination on the multiple appearances of the question.[7] It is a method that certainly influenced the priest scholar. Wojtyła learned much from Scheler's philosophy and sociology, but he concluded that his ideas did not provide a sound basis for Christian ethics as he placed too much emphasis on feeling, did not sufficiently emphasise conscience in human morality and had not recognised God explicitly as 'the exemplary being'.

For Wojtyła, it became ever clearer that you become the person you want to be by choice, by 'intentional will'. In his view, Scheler failed to perceive the basic truth, namely 'that the only value that can be called ethical value is a value that has the acting person as its efficient cause ... [Scheler's] whole interpretation deals only with secondary elements, which he tries ... to elevate to the primary level'.[8]

Nevertheless, Wojtyła acknowledged that his research into Scheler's work had benefited him greatly:

> My previous Aristotelian-Thomistic formation was enriched by the phenomenological method, and this made it possible for me to undertake a number of creative studies ... In this way I took part in the contemporary movement of philosophical personalism, and my studies were able to bear fruit in my pastoral work.[9]

Indeed, during his studies, he enjoyed existentialist philosophy and read the works of Jean-Paul Sartre extensively.

After completing his second doctoral thesis Wojtyła taught at the Theology Faculty of Jagiellonian University in Kraków, but he kept up his pastoral outreach. He had decided that he would study theology and philosophy but not 'forget' he was a priest.[10] Perhaps it's not exaggeration to say that he built up a new educational system. He would gather with students on their free days and go hiking and cycling to the Carpathian hills or to the lakes; they would discuss life's issues and often Wojtyła would celebrate Mass on a rock or on a canoe turned upside down to serve as an altar.

In 1956, Lublin became Wojtyła's principal academic base. At thirty-six years of age he was now the senior member of a faculty of the most important Catholic philosophical and theological centre of learning in Eastern Europe. His lectures covered the ethics of not only Scheler, but of Plato, Aristotle, Augustine, Aquinas and Kant, and were packed with students as a result. He also explored the utilitarian English philosophers, David Hume and Jeremy Bentham. Students enjoyed his teaching and often turned to him for advice and chats. His research continued and he even wrote a well-esteemed article on the compilation of Church laws by Gratian, the twelfth-century founder of the science of canon law. During 1957 and 1958 he composed an essay 'On Love and Responsibility', that would later be expanded and issued as a book.

In July 1958, Wojtyła was nominated as an auxiliary bishop in Kraków, choosing as his apostolic motto '*Totus tuus*' ('All yours') – a phrase taken from Louis-Marie Griginon de Montfort, saint and doctor of the Church whose book had influenced him earlier in life. Just one year later, Pope John XXIII made the surprising announcement that he was convoking a council of the world's bishops. The Second Vatican Council was to become the central source from which the young bishop, and later Pope, would draw abundantly.

The Second Vatican Council (1962–1965)
'My theology was formed at the Council'

In his last will and testament, published just days after his death, Pope John Paul described the Second Vatican Council (commonly known as Vatican II) as 'the key influence' throughout the twenty-six and a half years of his papacy. For the Catholic Church today, the Council continues to be the guiding compass.

It's easy to see why the Second Vatican Council was such a hugely important event in Karol Wojtyła's life. Some 2,300 bishops and five hundred theologian advisers attended, as well as observers from other churches, religions and lay auditors. By the end it had produced sixteen documents covering a whole range of subjects. But more than the numbers and outcomes, there is another reason why the Council probably made such an impact on the future Pope. In the first centuries of the Church it was often said that a Council acted as a powerful experience of Jesus present among those gathered in his name: 'where two or three are gathered in my name, I am there among them' (Mt 18:20). And what better setting, therefore, to think of God and of all things in God. With Jesus himself, 'the Teacher', among those assembled at Vatican II, it is little wonder that Pope John Paul commented that his theology was formed there.[11] Unsurprisingly, on becoming Pope he made it clear that the agenda for his pontificate was going to be the Council.

The famous phrase from John Paul II's first encyclical, *Redemptor Hominis*, that 'humanity is the way of the Church' was his way of expressing the Second Vatican Council's conviction that we need to link our notion of God and our understanding of what it is to be human.[12] He had learned the simple logic of the Council: if Jesus is the Son of God, the true image of God, then we who are created in the image and likeness of God come to fully understand not just God but ourselves when we look to Jesus Christ, the God-man. The question of what it is to be human revolves around the discovery that 'Jesus Christ is the principle way of the Church. He is our way to the home of the Father and he is the way of everyone.'[13]

There is one particular text from the Council that John Paul II would quote again and again: the 'Pastoral Constitution on the Church in the Modern World', *Gaudium et Spes* (a document he had helped prepare). The text clinches his conviction that in Jesus Christ we discover what it means to be human, and this is the 'anthropological revolution' that the Second Vatican Council underlined:

> The truth is that only in the mystery of the incarnate Word does the mystery of man take on light. For Adam, the first man, was a figure of him who was to come, namely Christ the Lord. Christ, the final Adam, by the revelation of the mystery of the Father and his love, fully reveals man to man himself and makes his supreme calling clear.[14]

To communicate God to others, the main thing to do is to follow the Son of God, who made himself one with us in all things but sin. The Church today must travel the way of making its own the 'joys and the hopes, the griefs and the anxieties of the people of this age', precisely because Jesus Christ 'has united himself in some fashion with everyone.'[15] This was a key conviction that John Paul took away from the Council.

What is amazing is that during what must have been a hectic time, the future Pope managed to multi-task at the Council, admitting that 'many parts of books and poems' were written during its four sessions.[16] For instance, it was at the Council that he had his first real contact with Africans, and on the margins of one of the official working documents he scribbled this poem, entitled 'The Negro':

> My dear brother, it's you, an immense land I feel
> where rivers dry up suddenly – and the sun
> burns the body as the foundry burns ore.
> I feel your thoughts like mind;
> if they diverge the balance is the same:
> in the scales truth and error.
> There is joy in weighing thoughts on the same scales,
> thoughts that differently flicker in your eyes and mine
> though their substance is the same.[17]

The young Polish bishop made something of a name for himself at the Council and the famous theologian, Henri de Lubac, commented very positively on him. Once it was concluded, Wojtyła returned to Poland and threw himself into making sure that the results of the Council would be well received, particularly regarding the mission of Christians in the world.[18] Little did he know that, less than fifteen years later, he would hear the senior Polish ecclesiastic, Cardinal Wyszyński, say to him at a Papal conclave: 'You will lead the Church into the third millennium.'[19]

Cardinal Karol Wojtyła
'Withstanding the trial of communism'

In his recently published work, *The End and the Beginning: Pope John Paul II – The Victory of Freedom, the Last Years, the Legacy,* George Weigel shows the magnitude of the communist war waged against Karol Wojtyła for almost forty years.[20] The KGB, the Polish Secret Police, and the East German Stasi were all involved. The tactics adopted included everything from blackmail plots to the assassination attempt of 1981.

Initially, however, when he was a priest lecturing at a university, the Polish authorities paid relatively little attention to Wojtyła. He was not considered an aggressive political type. Even after he was created cardinal on 28 June 1967, a report by the Polish Secret Police concluded that he represented 'open Catholicism', and that 'it seems that politics are his weaker suit; he is over-intellectualized ... He lacks organizing and leadership qualities, and this is his weakness in the rivalry with Wyszyński.'[21] But that mild verdict was to change as various acts began to show Wojtyła's increasing commitment to standing up for the truth in the face of an oppressive regime.

While lecturing in Lublin he had observed the ominous events, intimidations and arrests that were taking place around him under communism. Cardinal Wyszyński and Archbishop Baziak, for instance, were both imprisoned. In June 1954, workers in the industrial city of Poznań clashed with security forces. Fifty-four people were killed and over two hundred injured. Huge tension ensued: Moscow felt that Poland was threatening the whole Socialist project. But the Poles held their nerve. While different in temperament from Cardinal Wyszyński (Wojtyła was more interested in Marxism as an intellectual problem), the future Pope appreciated Wyszyński's wisdom and witness. Later he commented: 'There would not have been a Polish Pope on the throne of Peter if the faith of Cardinal Wyszyński had not been there, and his imprisonment and Jasna Góra.'[22]

As cardinal Wojtyła began campaigning for the building of churches – something that had been impeded by the authorities as a way of interfering with religious freedom. For years he struggled to get a church built in the workers' suburb of Nowa Huta, a place that had been created by the government as a 'socialist city'. This most famous

of modern churches in Poland was eventually consecrated in 1977.
Through homilies linking Polish history and Christianity, Cardinal
Wojtyła opposed the communist claim to be the true representative of
the Polish people. In 1971, after rioting workers were killed by army and
security troops at Gdańsk, the port city on the Baltic, he denounced the
bloodshed and demanded 'the right to bread, the right to freedom ... a
climate of real liberty ... of freedom from fear over what may happen if
one does this or that'.[23] The cardinal combined negotiation skills with
toughness in his dealings with the government and soon the regime
began to fear him:

> A man they had imagined to be a quite intellectual had
> become a charismatic public personality. His defence of
> religious freedom was increasingly sharp-edged and struck
> the regime at its most vulnerable point, its claim to be the
> true representative of the Polish people.[24]

Communism had become a powerful threat and a challenge to the
entire world. The cardinal persevered in countering its culture of lies,
despite all attempts to silence or block him. He could see the devastating
effects of its all-pervasive system. It claimed to have humanity at its
centre, but actually ended up obliterating the dignity of the human
person. It fragmented and atomised people – paradoxically to form new
socialist man – and produced a culture of oppression and fear, with the
party being promoted as everything.

What kept the cardinal zealous was his lively faith in God's
providence. He recalled how a young Flemish priest had once said to
him concerning Eastern Europe: 'The Lord allowed the experience of
such an evil as communism to affect you ... We were spared this in the
West, because perhaps we could not have withstood so great a trial.
You, on the other hand, can take it.' It was a remark that remained fixed
in Karol Wojtyła's memory: 'to some degree it had a prophetic value. I
often recall it and I see ever more clearly the accuracy of his diagnosis'.[25]

In the midst of withstanding personal and collective trials, the
cardinal's long-established interest in the human person took on a new
focus in the polemic against Marxism. Interest in the human person
and his or her dignity was growing because Marxists themselves had
made the question of humanity the centre of their arguments. Their
atheistic interpretations of reality, however, were one-sided, rejecting

the transcendent. Wojtyła was prepared to engage the Marxists in their ideology. He stated that though he did not write *The Acting Person* as a direct response to Marxism, 'the first to take notice of it, obviously in order to attack it, were the Marxists. In fact, my book represented an unsettling element in their polemic against religion and the Church.'[26] Furthermore, the questions young people were asking him in the context of post-war and communist Poland stirred reflections in him that would result in publications such as *Love and Responsibility*.

As cardinal, Karol Wojtyła wasn't only focussed on communism or on Poland. He kept before him the agenda of the Council, promoted the laity and welcomed new initiatives and movements. He attended synods in Rome, was appointed to the Pontifical Council for Laity and soon became familiar with new parts of the world – America and Canada, New Zealand and Australia, the Holy Land, Papua New Guinea and the Philippines. The Pole was a Pope in the making. Soon he would be 'called from a far country' to become the bishop of Rome on 16 October 1978.

2

Theological Foundations

'One duty of the Pope is to profess this truth and to render it present to the Church in Rome as well as to the entire Church, to all humanity, and to the whole world ... I would suggest a reading of Saint Augustine, who often repeated: "I am a bishop for you, I am a Christian with you".'

~ *Crossing the Threshold of Hope*

Jesus Christ the Redeemer of Humankind
'Do not be afraid! Open wide the doors for Christ!'

At the Mass to inaugurate his pontificate on 22 October 1978, Pope
John Paul uttered words that reverberated throughout his whole mission
as Pope:

> Do not be afraid to welcome Christ and accept his power
> ... Do not be afraid! Open wide the doors for Christ! To
> his saving power open the boundaries of states, economic
> and political systems, the vast fields of culture, civilization
> and development. Do not be afraid. [27]

He went on to explain: 'Christ knows "what is in man". He alone knows
it.' There could be no doubting that Pope John Paul saw his task as that
of pointing to Jesus Christ, 'the centre of the universe and of history',
because 'the decisive answer to every one of our questions, our religious
and moral questions in particular, is given by Jesus Christ, or rather is
Jesus Christ himself'.[28]

In his first encyclical, *Redemptor Hominis*, the Polish Pope
opened his heart and allowed a glimpse of his deep conviction of the
significance of Jesus Christ as Redeemer:

> It was to Christ the Redeemer that my feelings and my
> thoughts were directed on 16 October of last year, when,
> after the canonical election, I was asked: 'Do you accept?'
> I then replied: 'With obedience in faith to Christ, my Lord
> ... in spite of the great difficulties, I accept'. Today I wish to
> make that reply known publicly to all without exception ...[29]

John Paul's understanding of Jesus Christ was vast. On the one hand,
he followed St Paul, who expands our vision right to the cosmic
dimensions of Jesus Christ who is 'before all things' and in whom
'all things hold together' (Col 1:17). And, in a surprisingly modern
approach to the identity of Jesus, he highlighted the doctrine of the
Trinity and the anthropological significance of Jesus' life, death and

resurrection. We are so inclined to contemplate Jesus Christ in isolation but, in fact, his identity is totally relational because, as the Son of God, he has from all eternity lived in the divine communion of the Trinity. It is this Trinitarian life that he wants to communicate to us, so that we can truly be what we are in God's plan.

The Pope particularly admired John's Gospel as it highlights how Jesus, the Word Incarnate, was totally directed during his life towards the Father and towards us. Jesus' food was to do the will of the Father who had sent him to reach out to us (cf. Jn 4:34). John Paul often echoed the teaching of Vatican II that noted how:

> ... the Lord Jesus, when he prayed to the Father, "that all may be one ... as we are one" (John 17:21-22) opened up vistas closed to human reason, for he implied a certain likeness between the union of the divine Persons, and the unity of God's sons and daughters in truth and charity.[30]

What Jesus reveals is that we are called to share in and to 'live the life of the Trinity', three Divine Persons who are totally related to – and from – one another in total self-giving. Each of us, created in the image and likeness of God, cannot fully find ourselves except through a sincere gift of ourselves (Lk 17:33). That is the law of heaven to be lived on earth.

Pope John Paul wrote a triptych of Trinitarian encyclicals, starting in 1979 with *Redemptor Hominis* on Jesus as the Redeemer of humanity; followed in 1980 by a meditation on God the Father as merciful love, *Dives in Misericordia*; and finally, in 1986, on the Holy Spirit as the living principle of communion in *Dominum et Vivificantem*. He was the first Pope to write a trilogy on the three persons of the Trinity, bringing us to the heart of divine revelation and from there developing an anthropology – that is, an understanding of what it is to be human.

In his encyclical letter on moral teaching, *Veritatis Splendor*, Pope John Paul writes: 'Jesus' way of acting and his words, his deeds and his precepts constitute the moral rule of the Christian life.'[31] But clearly, Jesus Christ is not just a moral teacher or example. As Redeemer he is the One who has taken on all our darkness, sin, fears and estrangement from God and transformed it from within. That is why we are not to be afraid. Wherever we see sin and darkness, doubt, failure or confusion – in ourselves, in others, in the world around us – we can recognise Jesus the Redeemer who has taken all of this onto Himself and instilled grace and light, peace and confidence. Any suffering we experience can be united to Jesus', and then Jesus' redeeming, transforming power begins to work in and through us.

John Paul never tired of repeating that Jesus has united himself to every human being. The Paschal Mystery – that is, the death and resurrection of Jesus – is at work in everyone. And so John Paul coined what became one of the key phrases of his pontificate: 'humanity is the primary and fundamental way for the Church'.[32] With passion he would repeat:

> For, since Christ died for everyone, and since the ultimate human vocation is in fact one, and divine, we ought to believe that the Holy Spirit in a manner known only to God offers to everyone the possibility of being associated with this Paschal Mystery.[33]

In everyone we meet, therefore, the Spirit is present. In every adversity we encounter, Jesus' death and resurrection is at work.

God the Father, Rich in Mercy
'Mercy is Love's second name'

In the period before the Second World War, Sister Faustina (a Polish nun who, on 30 April 2000, would become the first saint in the third millennium to be canonised by John Paul) had been 'the herald of the one message capable of offsetting the evil of those ideologies [Nazism and communism], the fact that God is Mercy...' For this reason, John Paul explains: 'when I was called to the See of Peter, I felt impelled to hand on those experiences of a fellow Pole that deserve a place in the treasury of the universal Church'.[34] He was prompted to communicate to the world that he too had come to believe mercy to be the greatest of God's attributes.

In his encyclical letter *Dives in Misericordia*, he reflected at length on this theme. Many were struck by his exploration of the Old Testament terms for mercy.[35] On the one hand, he refers to the term *hesed*. Used in the Old Testament, this word implies a love that is merciful in the sense of fidelity: God is always faithful to the covenant he has entered into. On the other hand, the term *rahamim* denotes the love of a mother for her child (*rehem* = mother's womb). Pope John Paul writes of the feminine and masculine qualities of God's love. In another document, *Mulieris Dignitatem* (1988), John Paul also points out that if we want an analogy for God we need to look at both what's best about fatherhood *and* motherhood on this earth.[36]

In *Dives in Misericordia* John Paul offers a meditative commentary on the Prodigal Son (Lk 15:11-32), coining the memorable sentence: 'mercy is ... love's second name'.[37] It restores value, and promotes and draws good from all forms of evil in the world. He sees all this in the mercy parable:

> This love is able to reach down to every prodigal son, to every human misery, and above all to every form of moral misery, to sin. When this happens, the person who is the object of mercy does not feel humiliated, but rather found again and 'restored to value'. The father first and foremost expresses to him his joy that he has been 'found again' and

that he has 'returned to life'. This joy indicates a good that
has remained intact: even if he is a prodigal, a son does not
cease to be truly his father's son; it also indicates a good that
has been found again, which in the case of the prodigal son
was his return to the truth about himself. (6)

In God, Pope John Paul sees a harmony between merciful love and
justice:

Love, so to speak, conditions justice and, in the final
analysis, justice serves love. The primacy and superiority
of love vis-à-vis justice – this is a mark of the whole of
revelation – are revealed precisely through mercy ... Mercy
differs from justice, but is not in opposition to it. (4)

In presenting an encyclical on divine mercy, Pope John Paul is engaging
with what he considers central to the Second Vatican Council: re-
proposing the true face of God to today's humanity. As he puts it, 'the
more the Church's mission is centred upon humankind the more it must
be confirmed and actualized theocentrically, that is to say, be directed
in Jesus Christ to the Father' (1). The Council saw the need for a new
discovery of God. It saw as its task the proclamation of the Gospel that
shows God is not a threat to human freedom but its fulfilment, because
God is Love and Mercy. Divine love sets us free.

The Holy Spirit, the Lord, the Giver of Life
'You don't pray enough to the Holy Spirit'

A simple episode from Pope John Paul II's youth reveals the beginnings of a relationship with the Spirit. The young Karol had become an altar server but was obviously given to being a little distracted during the ceremonies: 'My father, having noticed my distraction said to me one day: you are not a good altar server. You don't pray enough to the Holy Spirit. You should pray to him. And he taught me a prayer.'[38] A particular closeness to the Spirit was to become one of the distinctive features of John Paul's teaching and prayer.

In describing the day of his ordination, he refers to the invocation of the *Veni Sancte Spiritus* as one of the most moving moments. Or again, when asked about how he prayed he would refer immediately to St Paul's Letter to the Romans: 'The Spirit too comes to the aid of our weakness; for we do not know how to pray as we ought, but the Spirit himself intercedes with inexpressible groaning' (cf. Rom 8:26). He was clearly someone who was very attentive to the voice of the Spirit within him. So, for instance, he explained his decision in 1986 to gather world religious leaders together to pray for peace in Assisi as an idea prompted by the Spirit.

But who is the Spirit? This question has intrigued theologians, mystics, and bishops throughout the centuries. Pope John Paul, following on from writers such as Thomas Aquinas, sees the Holy Spirit as Love. The Spirit is the personal expression of the mutual love and mutual self-giving of the Father and Son. He is the 'Person-Gift' in the Trinity, the Divine Person poured into the hearts of each of us at baptism and confirmation (cf. Rom 5:5). Not least for John Paul, the Spirit is 'the gift of the truth of conscience and the gift of the certainty of redemption.'[39]

In his encyclical on the Holy Spirit, *Dominum et Vivificantem*, Pope John Paul took up the Second Vatican Council's affirmation that the Church 'is in Christ like a sacrament or as a sign or instrument both of a very closely knit union with God and of the unity of the whole human race.'[40] But he went on to develop this notion in reference to the event

of Christ with its supreme gift of the Spirit. Born at the foot of the
Cross and made manifest at Pentecost, the Church is an event, brought
about by the Holy Spirit, of the continuous and ever-new coming of the
Crucified and Risen Jesus Christ into the hearts of the disciples and in
the midst of them united in his name.[41]

Accordingly, Pope John Paul went on to affirm that 'while it is an
historical fact that the Church came forth from the Upper Room on the
day of Pentecost', in a certain sense 'one can say that she has never left
it. Spiritually, the event of Pentecost does not belong only to the past:
the Church is always in the Upper Room that she bears in her heart.'[42] In
this sense, John Paul understood the Church to be always in a situation
of Pentecost, with new manifestations of that fact opening up all the
time throughout the Church's history. This explains why he emphasised
the charismatic dimension (expressed, for instance, in new movements
of renewal, monasticism, prophetic figures and saints) as 'co-essential' to
the hierarchical-sacramental side of the Church.

The Spirit is present in our lives, convinces us of sin and our need
of conversion. It is the Spirit who helps us overcome the slavery of sin
in all its forms and lead us to the freedom of the children of God. It is
the Spirit who gives us the gifts that empower us to live 'in Christ'. The
Spirit is not an alternative to Christ but always leads to Christ.

Pope John Paul's perspective is again vast. For him the Spirit's
presence and activity affects not only individuals but also society and
history, peoples, cultures and religions. The Spirit, who 'blows where
he wills' (cf. Jn 3:8), 'has filled the world' and 'holds all things together'
(Wis 1:7), is at the origin of the noble ideals and undertakings that
benefit humanity on its journey through history. John Paul was utterly
convinced that this Spirit is at work in every time and place: 'I have
repeatedly called this fact to mind, and it has guided me in my meetings
with a wide variety of peoples.'[43] He was convinced that 'every authentic
prayer is prompted by the Holy Spirit, who is mysteriously present in
every human heart'.[44] And right from his first encyclical he expressed
his conviction that the Church in our time seems to be repeating with
greater insistence and fervour: 'Come, Holy Spirit! Come! Come!'[45]

God's Plan of Salvation and the Mission of the Church
'One plan of unity that embraces everyone'

The date of 27 October 1986 can be numbered as one of the greatest days in Pope John Paul II's pontificate. Responding to his invitation, many leaders of the world's religions came together with him in Assisi, the Umbrian town of St Francis, to pray for peace. People knew something extraordinary was happening. Over eight hundred journalists turned up – even more than the five hundred who had attended Vatican II. There was an almost universally positive response to the event. As Pope John Paul later commented: 'This event seems to me to have been so significant that it invites us to reflect more deeply, in order to see ever more clearly its meaning.'[46]

In his own reflection, Pope John Paul recalled the conviction that was 'inculcated' in him by the teachings of the Second Vatican Council: God has one plan that embraces all of humanity. The Assisi event helped him to understand better that the true sense of the mission of the Church is to promote this one plan of unity and reconciliation.

As he put it, the Assisi event was a 'visible expression of the hidden but radical unity which the divine Word, "in whom everything was created, and in whom everything exists" (Col 1:16; Jn 1:3), has established among the men and women of this world'. This includes those of the twentieth century but also those who have gone before us in history and also those who will come after us.

Not denying the specific Judeo-Christian revelation in any way, but rather penetrating its deepest meaning, John Paul, clearly influenced by Vatican II but possibly also by theologians such as Henri de Lubac, commented:

> … there is only one divine plan for every human being
> who comes into this world (cf. Jn 1:9), one single origin
> and goal, whatever may be the colour of his or her skin,
> the historical and geographical framework within which
> he or she happens to live and act, or the culture in which
> he or she grows up and expresses him/herself. The

differences are a less important element, when compared
with the unity which is radical, fundamental and decisive.

In other words, everyone born into this world is embraced within God's
plan. Each of us shares in the divine origin of the whole human family
(see the Book of Genesis 1-2). Each of us bears the image of the Triune
God, and each of us is directed towards God, our common goal. The
Pope quotes Augustine to express the common quest for God written
into every human heart: 'You have made us for yourself, O' Lord and
our heart has no rest, until it rests in you.' For John Paul, the Assisi
meeting was 'a clear sign of the profound unity of all those who seek
in religion spiritual and transcendent values that respond to the great
questions of the human heart despite concrete divisions'.

The centre of this plan of God is Jesus Christ. Jesus has died for all and
the Holy Spirit gives to everyone the chance of coming into contact with
Jesus' death and resurrection 'in the way that God alone knows'. In fact,
we read in Scripture that God 'wills that all should be saved and come to
the knowledge of the truth. For there is only one God and one mediator
between God and humankind' (1 Tim 2:4-6). Even though unknown
to many, the fact is that Jesus 'has united himself in a certain manner to
everyone.'[47]

On this basis, Pope John Paul did not restrict or limit God to our
measures. There is an overarching plan of unity. Some of the differences
between us – peoples, cultures, religions – are the result of the genius and
spiritual riches that God has given to us in different ways. Some of the
differences come from the limitations and failures of the human spirit. But
all of this is taken up into God's plan. Jesus Christ is 'the Saviour of the
world' who 'died for all' (cf. Jn 4:42).

What then is the Church's identity in all of this? It is nothing less than
to be 'a sign and instrument of intimate union with God and of the unity
of the whole human race'. As the document on the Church in the Second
Vatican Council put it: 'This means that the Church is called to work
with all her energies … so that the wounds and divisions of humankind –
which separate them from their origin and goal, and make them hostile to
one another – may be healed.'

Again, John Paul II's outlook is expansive. He considers that the entire
human race, in the infinite complexity of its history, with its different
cultures, is 'called to form the new People of God' in which 'the blessed

union of God with humankind and the unity of the human family are healed, consolidated and raised up'. Quoting the Second Vatican Council, he affirms:

> All are called to be part of this Catholic unity of the people of God which in promoting universal peace presages it. And there belong to or are related to it in various ways, the Catholic faithful, all who believe in Christ, and indeed the whole of mankind, for all are called by the grace of God to salvation.[48]

Perhaps we don't normally 'see this real orientation of all people towards the unity of the one People of God'. It took an event like Assisi to show it and to help Christians further understand their communion with one another. There 'the profound communion which already exists between us in Christ and in the Spirit, a communion that is living and active even if as yet incomplete' was manifested. In the town of St Francis, Pope John Paul came to a new appreciation of how the Church is called to be the seed of unity and hope for all humanity.

The Dignity of the Human Person
'Two wings on which to contemplate the Truth'

For many, safeguarding humanity and its place in the cosmos can only come through marginalising God, denying any dimension that transcends this world and its historical dimensions. Karol Wojtyła, who had lived through wars and repressive regimes, wanted to affirm that it is not only possible but necessary to hold together theocentrism (focus on God) and anthropocentrism (focus on humankind). Having witnessed totalitarian regimes, he understood that if we get rid of God or the transcendent dimension, then humankind's dignity and freedom – and the earth itself – are devastated.

Since Descartes, what it is to be human has been overly identified with primarily cognitive functions. Metaphysics has been downplayed and focus has been on the philosophy of knowledge. Famously, the French philosopher wrote *'cogito, ergo sum'* ('I think, therefore I am'), but the human being is more than just thinking. Men and women make decisions, make a stand on issues, and they act in relation to life in all its aspects.

In his famous play, *The Jeweller's Shop*, Wojtyła presents the character of Andrew, who recalls the jeweller's description of the human being:

> Ah, the proper weight of man!
> This rift, this tangle, this ultimate depth –
> this clinging, when it is so hard
> to unstuck heart and thought.
> And in all this – freedom,
> a freedom, and sometimes frenzy,
> the frenzy of freedom trapped in this tangle.
> And in all this – love,
> which springs from freedom,
> as water springs from an oblique rift in the earth.
> This is man![49]

When he had completed the first draft of his key philosophical work, *The Acting Person*, the bishop philosopher wrote to the theologian Henri de Lubac describing his study as:

A work that is close to my heart and devoted to the
metaphysical sense and mystery of the PERSON. It seems
to me that the debate today is being played out at that
level. The evil of our times consists in the first place in
a kind of degradation, indeed in a pulverization, of the
fundamental uniqueness of each human person ... To this
disintegration planned at times by atheistic ideologies,
we must oppose, rather than sterile polemics, a kind of
'recapitulation' of the inviolable mystery of the person.[50]

If *The Acting Person* deals with Wojtyła's anthropology, his fundamental
vision of what it is to be human, another of his works, *Love and
Responsibility*, deals with that anthropology's ethical application and
development.

All of this is the background to Pope John Paul II's strenuous
defence of the dignity of the human being – of every human being as a
unique, unrepeatable person directed towards truth, goodness and love.
We find this particular focus on anthropological questions in three of his
encyclicals: *Veritatis Splendor* (1993), *Evangelium Vitae* (1995) and *Fides
et Ratio* (1998). As Maciej Zięba puts it, the human person for John
Paul is not 'like a fly caught up in a spider-web of economic, political,
and techno-medialogical determinants which effectively render him
or her a pawn of impersonal structures and mechanisms'.[51] The human
being is more than simply biology. The world is more than just scientific
data. We are made to ask the 'big questions' about life and our world, its
meaning and its direction.

Starting, as he so often does, with faith in creation, the Pope links his
exploration of anthropological issues with a God-centred focus.

Reason draws its own truth and authority from the
eternal law, which is none other than divine wisdom
itself ... The natural law is nothing other than the light of
understanding infused in us by God.[52]

The Christian proclamation is very much linked with the affirmation of the
dignity of the human being who is directed towards Truth in itself. Faith
is not opposed to reason but can stimulate it to strive for the great things
for which it was created. Commenting on John Paul's thought, Cardinal

Ratzinger took up Kant's expression *'sapere aude'* ('dare to know') and
proposed that:

> ... we could affirm that the Pope is calling once again on
> reason that no longer dares at a metaphysical level: *sapere
> aude!* Dare! It is to this you are destined! The Pope shows
> that faith will not reduce reason to silence but will free it
> from the veil that covers it and blocks it from facing the big
> questions of humanity.[53]

For John Paul, faith defends humanity in its reality of being human.
Faith today is called to help reason dare to affirm the truth. As he puts
it in *Fides et Ratio*: 'There is thus no reason for competition of any kind
between reason and faith: each contains the other, and each has its own
scope for action.'[54] Without reason faith collapses; without faith reason
risks atrophying. And the human person is at risk.

His reflection also leads him to intervene in the area of moral theology
that had, in a certain sense, run aground in the 1960s and 70s after an
initial positive renewal in the light of Scripture and on the basis of salvation
history. It had encountered the difficulty of how to respond to concrete
issues faced by the modern world. Just quoting the Bible was no longer
enough. For some, however, natural law was an outdated notion. Others
felt we could no longer recognise something as good or evil in itself – that
the most that might be said, on the basis of calculations of consequences, is
that one thing is better than another. This direction in moral theology risked
dissolving morality altogether, as the good in itself was no longer deemed
to exist. The Bible was considered to be, at best, an inspiring motivation but
devoid of moral norms. It is against this tendency that the Pope sought to
re-establish the legitimacy of a metaphysical vision that derives from faith in
creation.[55]

Sustaining the possibility of a metaphysics on the basis of creation, Pope
John Paul II believed that we can understand the Bible's word as relevant to
the many issues we face daily – that there can be a biblical ethics that guides
us towards the Truth for which we have been created. This guided him in his
reflection on moral theology in the Church. His anthropological concern
was clear: if we cannot know the truth, then all that we do and think is
simply convention or opinion, tradition or the mere result of a calculation of
consequences.

On a more general level, John Paul wanted to remind everyone that:

> Faith and reason are like two wings on which the human
> spirit rises to the contemplation of truth; and God has placed
> in the human heart a desire to know the truth – in a word,
> to know himself – so that, by knowing and loving God, men
> and women may also come to the fullness of truth about
> themselves.[56]

His social encyclicals were an unfolding of this conviction.

Mary, Mother of God, Mother of the Church
'Would Mary detract from the place due to Jesus in my life?'

Pope John Paul's devotion to Mary is well known. Avery Dulles has commented that it would, however, be a mistake to think of it as the fruit of sentimentality. On the contrary, he had a deep theological and spiritual understanding of Mary's central place in the whole plan of salvation that centres on Jesus Christ.[57] During his pontificate he delivered a staggering number of Marian sermons, as well as weekly Angelus messages and encyclicals dedicated to Marian themes.

His own personal story with Mary, the Mother of God, has a simple beginning. Karol Wojtyła grew up admiring the image of Our Lady of Perpetual Help in his parish church of Wadowice. His parents brought him on frequent pilgrimages to Marian shrines, such as the shrine of Jasna Góra with its Black Madonna in Czestochowa, and as a teenager he became a member of a young people's Living Rosary Movement that prayed for peace and liberation.[58]

However, at a certain point, the young Wojtyła went through something of a minor crisis: would Mary detract from the place that was due to Jesus in his life? It was one of those questions the Holy Spirit puts into a heart because he wants to offer a response. Wojtyła found the answer to his question in the classic work of Louis-Marie Grignion de Montfort, *True Devotion to the Blessed Virgin Mary*, and reading it marked a 'decisive turning-point' in his life. In it, he discovered a Marian devotion that was based completely on Jesus Christ, the Incarnation and Redemption.

It was not enough for him to read de Montfort's work once – it became part of his life. Years later, he recalled having carried a copy of the book with him for a long time, even to the chemical plant where he worked, with the result that its handsome binding became spotted with lime.[59]

From then on, the future Pope's love of Mary, the Mother of Our Lord, sprang from the very heart of the Trinity and Jesus Christ. It deepened into an intellectual vision that would eventually also incorporate his developing insights into the Church and the human person, the world and the course of history. It bore fruit also in the encyclical *Redemptoris Mater* (1987) and the apostolic letters *Mulieris Dignitatem* (1988) and *Rosarium Virginis Mariae* (2002).

There is much that could be said about John Paul's understanding of Mary's place in God's plan. He reflects, for instance, on her pilgrimage of faith as the first disciple of her Son and underlines how her special position did not exempt her from travelling the ups and downs of the spiritual journey of discipleship. In particular, he proposes the relevancy of her faith journey, the 'Way of Mary', as he calls it, for all who want to follow Jesus.

Stefano De Fiores, the renowned Italian Mariologist, points out that the way John Paul II highlights Mary's faith journey both responds to some of the feminist demands to recognise Mary as a centre of decision and responsibility, and is at the same time attentive to the Protestant concern not to detract from the affirmation of Christ as the one Mediator.[60]

Among the many biblical meditations offered by the Pope, one topic comes up repeatedly: Mary's experience at the foot of the Cross (Jn 19:25). It's the moment when she who has cooperated throughout Jesus' mission, shares in the shocking mystery of his self-emptying. 'This is perhaps the deepest *kenosis* [emptying] of faith in human history.'[61] But it is at this moment that the dying Jesus entrusts Mary to John and John (representing humanity) to Mary, thus bestowing upon her a new, expanded and universal motherhood (Jn 19:25-27) (23).

Mary's maternity is perhaps *the* major theme in John Paul's Mariological and, in some ways, in is ecclesiological teaching. While the Second Vatican Council spoke of Mary as model of the Church, John Paul II also emphasises how 'Mary, herself, then, through her own everlasting motherhood "cooperates in the birth and development of the sons and daughters of Mother Church"' (44).

Following de Montfort's invitation, John Paul also suggests that we cast ourselves into the 'mould' of Mary as a simpler way of progressing in our spiritual life. Having cast himself into this mould, with his motto '*Totus Tuus*', John Paul II sought simply to love and live each present moment imitating and entrusting himself to Mary. And in this way he let the Almighty God do great things.

3

Spirituality

'Is it not one of the "signs of the times" that in today's world, despite
widespread secularisation, there is a widespread demand for
spirituality?'

~ *Novo Millennio Ineunte*

Conversion as a Permanent Attitude
'Believe in God's merciful love'

Love is more powerful than death; it is more powerful than sin. Love is patient and kind; it never comes to an end. It was believing that God's love is behind all circumstances that characterised John Paul's life – even in the face of an assassination attempt: 'Ağca knew how to shoot, and he certainly shot to kill. Yet it was as if someone was guiding and deflecting that bullet ... I was in pain ... but I had a strange trust.'[62]

As has already been noted, the particular attribute of love that John Paul highlighted was mercy – 'love's second name', as he put it. That mercy flowed from the Crucified Christ. In looking to him we can start 'believing that love is present in the world and that this love is more powerful than any kind of evil in which individuals, humanity, or the world are involved. Believing in this love means believing in mercy' in the face of all our limits, sinfulness, fears and oppressions at every level – personal, social, institutional.[63]

How many times in his life Karol Wojtyła must have had to renew his belief in God's merciful love! We can only imagine what the successor of Peter must have gone through to persevere in his faith until the end. He hints at some of his interior drama when he writes of Peter who said, 'depart from me, Lord, for I am a sinful man' (Lk 5:8). There must have been testing times, not least during the months after the assassination attempt.

Pope John Paul gave witness to his faith when he reminded us that Christ knows what is in our heart (cf. Jn 2:25) and that there is no evil from which God cannot draw forth a greater good. There is no suffering which he cannot transform into a path leading to him.

To live in the knowledge that one is an object of God's merciful love prompts constant conversion. It is an attitude to cultivate in life:

> Authentic knowledge of the God of mercy, the God of
> tender love, is a constant and inexhaustible source of
> conversion ... a permanent attitude ... a state of mind.
> Those who come to know God in this way, who 'see' Him

in this way, can live only in a state of being continually
converted to Him ... and it is this state of conversion
which marks out the most profound element of the
pilgrimage of every man and woman on earth ... [64]

By believing in God's merciful love, entrusting everything unto God,
living with the freedom of the children of God, we go out 'to practice
mercy' towards others: 'Blessed are the merciful, for they shall obtain
mercy' (Mt 5:7):

Mercy that is truly Christian is also, in a certain sense, the
most perfect incarnation of 'equality' between people ...
'equality' of people through 'patient and kind' love does
not take away differences: the person who gives becomes
more generous when he feels at the same time benefited
by the person accepting his gift; and vice versa, the person
who accepts the gift with the awareness that, in accepting
it, he too is doing good is in his own way serving the great
cause of the dignity of the person; and this contributes to
uniting people in a more profound manner. [65]

The sense of being an 'unworthy servant', but enveloped by merciful
love so characterised John Paul that towards the end of his life he was
able to say: 'the sense of being an "unworthy servant" is growing in me
in the midst of all that happens around me – and I think I feel at ease
with this'. [66]

Learning from the Eucharist
'The Eucharist provides the plan for mission'

During the retreat he gave to Pope Paul VI and his close co-workers in the Vatican Curia during Lent 1976, the future Pope emphasised with passion the need to recall and repeat to people that Jesus Christ is with us: 'His love for you is so great that he gave himself fully and irrevocably. Jesus wished us to inherit from him nothing less than love of every single human being.'[67] It is above all in the Eucharist that Jesus Christ communicates this love to us.

Pope John Paul II spent his life meditating on the great mystery of the Eucharist under three headings: the Eucharist as sacrifice, communion and real presence. In 2004, in his apostolic letter for the year of the Eucharist, *Mane Nobiscum Domine*, we are given an insight into the Pope's meditation and his conviction of Christ's presence in the Eucharist.[68]

He starts by reflecting on the episode of the two disciples journeying to Emmaus on the evening of the day of the resurrection. They are weighed down with sadness. But then Someone joins them in conversation. They initially don't recognise that it is the Risen Jesus. But he brings light into their darkness; he rekindles their hope. John Paul comments, '"Stay with us," they pleaded. And he agreed. Soon afterwards, Jesus' face would disappear, yet the Master would "stay" with them, hidden in the "breaking of the bread" which had opened their eyes to recognize him.'[69]

For Pope John Paul, this is the great encounter we have each time we attend Mass. Jesus Christ is really present – in his body, his blood, his soul and his divinity:

> This presence ... is called 'real' not in an exclusive way, as if to suggest that other forms of Christ's presence are not real, but *par excellence*, because Christ thereby becomes substantially present, whole and entire, in the reality of his body and blood ... The Eucharist is a mystery of presence with us until the end of the world. (16)

To appreciate the greatness of the Mass we need eyes of faith. It can be easy to notice only the external elements – the bread and wine, the priest, the prayers, the songs – but faith brings us to believe that the celebration of the Eucharist is a very particular encounter with Jesus Christ. Pope John Paul refers us to Rublëv's celebrated icon of the Trinity which 'clearly places the Eucharist at the centre of the life of the Trinity' (11). In that icon, the Holy Spirit is depicted on the left-hand side, Jesus at the centre, and the Father on the right. The Holy Spirit and Jesus have their faces turned towards the Father, who returns their gaze. Jesus, at the centre, has two fingers extended, indicating his two natures. In the middle of the table, in front of the figures, is a vessel containing the sacrificial lamb, representing the mystery of the Eucharist.

Pope John Paul reminds us that we need to let our minds be enlightened and our hearts enkindled in love if we are to understand what is going on in the Eucharist. The disciples on the road to Emmaus recognised Jesus in the breaking of the bread because 'when minds are enlightened and hearts are enkindled, signs begin to "speak" ... Through these signs the mystery in some way opens up before the eyes of the believer' (14).

There are certain conditions that permit the opening of our eyes. Pope John Paul comments, for instance, on the need to live the mutual love that is the heart of fellowship expressed in the Eucharist:

> The Eucharist was born, on the evening of Holy Thursday,
> in the setting of the Passover meal. *Being a meal* is part
> of its very structure. 'Take, eat ... Then he took a cup
> and ... gave it to them, saying: Drink from it, all of you'
> (Mt 26:26, 27). As such, it expresses the fellowship God
> wants to establish with us and which we ourselves must
> build with one another. (15)

It is important to enter into the dynamic of dying and rising with Jesus Christ:

> Yet it must not be forgotten that the Eucharistic meal
> also has a profoundly and primarily *sacrificial* meaning.
> In the Eucharist, Christ makes present to us anew *the*
> *sacrifice offered once for all on Golgotha*. Present in the

Eucharist as the Risen Lord, he nonetheless bears the
marks of his passion, of which every Mass is a 'memorial',
as the Liturgy reminds us in the acclamation following
the consecration: 'We announce your death, Lord, we
proclaim your resurrection'... (15)

The Eucharist also invites us to keep hope alive within us, living already
in the realisation that, in Christ, we are being directed towards God the
Father:

At the same time, while the Eucharist makes present
what occurred in the past, it also *impels us towards the
future, when Christ will come again* at the end of history.
This 'eschatological' aspect makes the Sacrament of the
Eucharist an event which draws us into itself and fills our
Christian journey with hope. (15)

Pope John Paul II reminds us what the Eucharistic mystery does. It
builds up the Church, modelled on the unity of the Trinity. It's not just
about our individual salvation. Since the Eucharist also manifests and
expresses ecclesial communion, it is for this reason 'the Church sets
conditions for full participation in the celebration of the Eucharist'
(n. 20–1). The Eucharist gives us an ideal against which to measure
ourselves:

At each Holy Mass we are called to measure ourselves
against the ideal of communion which the *Acts of the
Apostles* paints as a model for the Church in every age. It
is the Church gathered around the Apostles, called by the
word of God, capable of sharing in spiritual goods but in
material goods as well (cf. Acts 2:42-7; 4:32-5). (22)

Finally, the Eucharist sends us out on mission, 'sensing the duty to be a
missionary of the event made present in that rite'. Indeed the Eucharist
provides the plan for mission:

For the Eucharist is a mode of being, which passes from
Jesus into each Christian, through whose testimony it is

meant to spread throughout society and culture. For this
to happen, each member of the faithful must assimilate,
through personal and communal meditation, the values
which the Eucharist expresses, the attitudes it inspires, the
resolutions to which it gives rise. (2)

Promoting the Spirituality of Communion
'Make the Church the school and home of communion'

The closing of the 'Holy Door' of St Peter's Basilica in Rome on 6 January 2001 marked the conclusion of the Jubilee Year 2000. It was moving to see the then-ageing Pope solemnly proceed in procession to a packed St Peter's square. As he walked out, he paused for a moment. It was as if he was looking beyond the crowd present in front of him and saying to himself: 'The celebrations are over, the second millennium of the Church is past, now let's look ahead to the new millennium.' In fact, over thirty-three million pilgrims had visited Rome, including around five million for the World Youth Day.

That same day, at the end of the Mass, Pope John Paul signed an apostolic letter, *Novo Millennio Ineunte (At the Beginning of the New Millennium)*. In it he expressed his deep conviction 'To make the Church *the home and the school of communion*: that is the great challenge facing us in the millennium which is now beginning.'[70] And so a spirituality of communion needs to be lived and promoted. He spoke of the great risk of running ahead in trying to do all kinds of things to benefit the Church. Many kinds of programmes and schemes could be devised that would undoubtedly be useful in their own way, but ultimately the basic programme remains the essential one given by Jesus: 'love one another as I have loved you ... By this all will know you are my disciples.' If the Church has mutual love it has everything. Without it, it has little of what it thinks it has.

In his very fine description of communion in terms of mutual love, Pope John Paul explains key features of this communitarian spirituality that is at the root of all vocations in the Church and the heart of all authentic renewal.[71]

First of all it involves 'the heart's contemplation of the mystery of the Trinity dwelling in us, and whose light we must also be able to see shining on the face of the brothers and sisters around us.'[72] This means sharing that one glance of our heart on the mystery of the Trinity that dwells within us and in which, through grace, we already in some way share in our mutual relations with one another: 'No one has greater love than this, to lay down one's life for one's friends' (Jn 15:13).

A spirituality of communion also means 'an ability to think of our brothers and sisters in faith within the profound unity of the Mystical Body, and therefore as "those who are a part of me"'. Here the Pope underlines the new 'thinking' and 'feeling' we need in terms of sharing with others 'their joys and sufferings ... their desires and ... their needs' (43). This means offering deep and genuine friendship. John Paul II, who is said to have met more people than any other human being, knew what he was talking about.

The spirituality of communion also implies 'the ability to see what is positive in others, to welcome it and prize it as a gift from God: not only as a gift for the brother or sister who has received it directly, but also as a "gift for me"' (43). We have been created as a gift for the person next to us and the person next to us has been created as a gift for us. Pope John Paul lived that out.

Finally, the Pope pointed to another pillar in the spirituality of communion that is so much needed if we are to be regenerated as people who create renewed relationships in the Church, at every level of its life and activity: to know how to 'make room' for our brothers and sisters, bearing each other's burdens (Gal 6:2) and resisting the selfish temptations which constantly beset us and provoke competition, careerism, distrust and jealousy.

The spirituality of communion would be a utopia were it not based on what John Paul called the 'mystery within the mystery' – Jesus Crucified and Forsaken (22). To build up communion means heeding Paul's Letter to the Philippians, which states that we need to adopt the 'emptying' that Jesus showed us in his Paschal Mystery in our relationships with one another:

> ... be of the same mind, having the same love, being in full
> accord and of one mind ... Let the same mind be in you
> that was in Christ Jesus, who, though he was in the form
> of God, did not regard equality with God as something
> to be exploited, but emptied himself, taking the form of a
> slave, being born in human likeness. And being found in
> human form, he humbled himself and became obedient to
> the point of death – even death on a cross (Phil 2:5-8).

The Pope was so convinced of this need for the widespread exercise of a spirituality of communion that he remarked with striking words: 'Let us have no illusions: unless we follow this spiritual path, external structures of communion will serve very little purpose. They would become mechanisms without a soul, "masks" of communion rather than its means of expression and growth' (43).

Listening to the Voice of the Spirit
'The Pope prays as the Holy Spirit permits him to pray'

When asked about how he prayed, Pope John Paul would respond by quoting St Paul's Letter to the Romans: 'The Spirit too comes to the aid of our weakness; for we do not know how to pray as we ought, but the Spirit himself intercedes with inexpressible groaning' (Rom 8:26). Anyone who witnessed him pray in the silence of his oratory will have heard something like a 'groaning' almost in unison with that of the Spirit. As he put it, 'The Pope prays as the Holy Spirit permits him to pray.'[73]

Sometimes it might seem that the starting point in prayer is what *we* want to say to God. But that is not the case. John Paul emphasises how our prayer begins with *God* within us. For him, God is not way up beyond the clouds in remote majesty and might. The great and distinctive feature of Christian faith is that, through grace, we have been brought into God – that is, into nothing less than Jesus Christ's prayer to the Father. For Pope John Paul it was 'a beautiful and salutary thought that wherever people are praying in the world, there the Holy Spirit is, the living breath of prayer'.[74] Through the Spirit we are 'in Christ' and Jesus Christ in us, in the power of the Spirit, prays to the Father.

So John Paul writes: 'We must pray with "inexpressible groaning" in order to enter into rhythm with the Spirit's own entreaties.'[75] We achieve 'the fullness of prayer not when we express ourselves, but when we let God be more fully present in our prayer'.[76] He points us to the great experts in prayer, the mystics such as Francis of Assisi, Teresa of Avila, John of the Cross, Ignatius of Loyola and Serafim of Sarov.

Prayer for John Paul is never simply an individual act. Our conversation with God 'within the Trinity' is always representative of creation and humanity. That's why in our prayer we take up the joys, hopes and anguish of people around us, the people of our time. Every Christian, carrying the world in his or her arms, as it were, is bound to strive for the victory of love, goodness and justice in the world and so pray for the world. Our prayer is always linked to the prayer of the Church for the salvation of all humankind.

In a powerful glimpse into his personal prayer, the Pope once described how in his time of prayer he followed a certain 'geography' of the whole world, 'a geography of communities, churches, societies, and also of the problems that trouble the world today'.[77] We can almost imagine him sitting, kneeling or prostrated on the floor, as he passed through his mind's eye the different situations, people and events that made up his universal prayer. Prompted by the Spirit, he brought them to mind so that he could put them into the heart of Jesus who is always directed towards God the Father.

In prayer, God reveals himself as the love that goes out to those who are suffering, supporting and uplifting us, and inviting us to trust. Many have remarked that to see Pope John Paul II in prayer, was to see a man 'immersed in God'. Cardinal Martins, for instance, who worked closely alongside the Pope in the Vatican, describes how he sometimes had to go to the Pope for a working lunch. Before going into the dining room they would visit the Blessed Sacrament in his private chapel with the other guests:

> I was always very impressed by the fact that when we were in the chapel, he knelt down and really immersed himself in God, and remained there not for a second or ten seconds, but for a long time, really immersed in God. I always admired the Pope's intensity of prayer.[78]

Recognising the Gospel of Suffering
'Love is the richest source of the meaning of suffering'

The theme of suffering in life is one that engaged Karol Wojtyła from his earliest years. As early as 1940 he wrote a play entitled *Job*, that in so many ways captures the cry of humankind when faced with pain and suffering, doubt and desolation. Why suffering? Why limits? Why death? Why does evil exist in the world? He refers again to Job in his 1984 apostolic letter on the Christian meaning of human suffering, *Salvifici Doloris*, stating that 'the Book of Job ... in a certain way is a foretelling of the Passion of Christ'.[79]

Contemplating the face of the Crucified and Risen Christ was the heart of John Paul's spirituality. It is there that he discovered the mysterious 'why' of suffering – in taking it onto Himself, Jesus Christ, the Son of God, reveals to us that 'Love is the richest source of the meaning of suffering.' The fact is that 'God so loved the world that he gave his only Son' (Jn 3:16). If there is someone the Father loves it is his own Son. And yet that Son suffered, so there must be a meaning in suffering.

In looking on the face of the Crucified and Risen Christ, John Paul meditated particularly on that moment when Jesus cried out on the Cross: 'My God, my God, why have you forsaken me?' (Mk 15:34). As John Paul asks, 'is it possible to imagine a greater agony, a more impenetrable darkness?'[80] The Pope knows this is not the anguished cry of a man without hope, but the prayer of the Son who offers his life to the Father in love, for the salvation of all. The very moment when Jesus identified fully with our sin, 'abandoned' by the Father, he abandoned himself into the hands of the Father and was raised up in the Resurrection. It is this dynamic of dying and rising in imitation of Jesus Crucified and Risen that John Paul proposes as the secret of life in his teaching.

To unite your suffering with that of Jesus Christ is to enter into profound encounter with the mystery of redemption. John Paul brings us right into the depths of the mystery of Jesus' suffering and abandonment on the Cross:

> One can say that these words on abandonment are born
> at the level of that inseparable union of the Son with the
> Father, and are born because the Father 'laid on him the
> iniquity of us all'. They also foreshadow the words of Saint
> Paul: 'For our sake he made him to be sin who knew no
> sin.' Together with this horrible weight, *encompassing the
> 'entire' evil of the turning away from God* which is contained
> in sin, Christ, through the divine depth of his filial union
> with the Father, perceives in a humanly inexpressible way
> *this suffering which is the separation,* the rejection *by the
> Father,* the estrangement from God. But precisely through
> this suffering he accomplishes the Redemption, and can
> say as he breathes his last: 'It is finished'.[81]

In the light of Jesus' death and resurrection, it can be believed that the
weaknesses of all human sufferings are capable of being infused with
the same power of God manifested in Christ's Cross. And therefore,
'In such a concept, *to suffer* means to become particularly *susceptible,*
particularly *open to the working of the salvific powers of God,* offered to
humanity in Christ' (23). John Paul explains: 'Christ through his own
salvific suffering is very much present in every human suffering, and can
act from within that suffering by the power of his Spirit of truth' (26).

The Pope, himself acquainted with suffering, brings us to see how it
can be a participation in the Church's mission:

> Christ has in a sense opened his own redemptive suffering
> to all human suffering. In so far as man becomes a sharer
> in Christ's sufferings – in any part of the world and at any
> time in history – to that extent *he in his own way completes*
> the suffering through which Christ accomplished the
> Redemption of the world. (24)

In the words of the Letter to the Colossians: 'I am completing what
is lacking in Christ's afflictions for the sake of his body, that is, the
Church (Col 1:24). But Jesus Crucified and Risen is not just the key to
our personal sufferings. He is also to be discovered in outreach to our
neighbour. Looking at Jesus we learn to forget ourselves and focus on
others:

The parable of the Good Samaritan belongs to the Gospel
of suffering. For it indicates what the relationship of each
of us must be towards our suffering neighbour. We are
not allowed to 'pass by on the other side' indifferently;
we must 'stop' beside him. *Everyone who stops beside the
suffering of another person*, whatever form it may take, is a
Good Samaritan. (28)

A Good Samaritan is a person capable of giving themselves to the neighbour who is suffering. On the basis of the Last Judgement of Matthew's Gospel, John Paul reminds us that whatever we do to our neighbour is done to Jesus Christ, who says, 'You did it to me':

He himself is the one who in each individual experiences
love; he himself is the one who receives help, when this
is given to every suffering person without exception. He
himself is present in this suffering person ... (30)

During an Angelus Message, on Sunday 29 May 1994, John Paul offered a very personal glimpse into his thoughts following a recent hospital stay:

I understand that I have to lead Christ's Church into this
third millennium by prayer, by various programs, but I
saw that this is not enough: she must be led by suffering
... the Pope has to suffer, so that every family may see
that there is, I would say, a higher Gospel: the Gospel of
suffering by which the future is prepared ... Again I have
to meet the powerful of the world and I must speak. With
what arguments? I am left with the subject of suffering.
And I want to tell them: understand it, think it over![82]

Contemplating and Living the Rosary
'The Rosary has an important place in my spiritual life'

There can be little doubt that the Rosary was John Paul II's favourite prayer. It sustained him not least throughout the horrors of World War II and again following the assassination attempt of 1981. We can only imagine how intensely he prayed it while undertaking the onerous, delicate and often dangerous tasks he had to perform during his years as Pope. For him the Rosary prayer was like David's catapult against giants! It helped him see light in the darkness.

On 16 October 2002, he issued an apostolic letter on the Rosary, *Rosarium Virginis Mariae*. In doing so he explained that he was building on *Novo Millennio Ineunte*, which had made a great impact two years previously. In that letter the Pope had written in radical terms of the need for all of us to 'start afresh from Christ'.[83] He calls the letter on the Rosary its 'complement'. It's as if the Pope was saying that if we want to start again from Christ, head of the mystical body the Church, we also need to start again from the other 'head' of the Church, the first disciple, the mother, the one 'who lives only in Christ and in view of Christ': Mary.

The feminine heart of the Church is vital. John Paul was utterly convinced of this, not least in view of the New Evangelisation. The Church is not just an organisation that gets things done. It is not just an institution following a fixed programme. It is not just the hierarchical structures that mediate Christ through sacramental grace and apostolic preaching. The Church is, above all, a way of life that Jesus communicated to us. And we have been given a model for that life – the woman who brought Jesus into the world. It is by living Mary that we live Christ.

With its strongly biblical perspective, its Christocentric focus and Trinitarian rhythm, the Pope's letter on the Rosary is crafted in an ecumenically sensitive manner. Mary is portrayed as leaving all the room and glory to Jesus, the Father and Holy Spirit. What John Paul shows us is that Mary *is* by *not being*. She is depicted as holding nothing for herself – neither the words directed to her nor the love that one can feel for her.[84] In the Pope's writing, as soon as he mentions Mary, she disappears, as it were, in God. She is the model from whom we can learn how to be the nothingness of love, full of God.

The letter on the Rosary speaks about the prayer 'of' Mary. It invites us to pray 'like' Mary. And it explains how it is we pray 'with' Mary. It suggests that by contemplating Christ with the eyes of Mary we pray, figuratively speaking, in Mary. In another context, the Archbishop of Canterbury, Rowan Williams also comments that when we echo Mary's 'yes', the vitality of God in Jesus Christ flows out from the centre of our being.[85]

By adding the five new 'Mysteries of Light' (The Baptism of Our Lord, The Wedding Feast of Cana, The Preaching of the Kingdom of God, The Transfiguration and the Institution of the Eucharist), John Paul II reminded us that Christ meets us as 'Light' and as a way of life that is light. He proposes the new mysteries be recited on Thursday (Saturday now being dedicated to the Joyful Mysteries).

At a time when 'experience' is highly valued, the Pope offers his spiritual experience in *Rosarium Virginis Mariae*. As people are turning to Oriental religions with mantras, beads, symbols and contemplation techniques, the Pope sets forth the Rosary as an authentic school of prayer to be rediscovered.[86]

In meditating the Rosary we learn to see and feel, love and think, suffer and live like Jesus Christ. In meditating the Rosary we bring to our prayer not only our problems and anxieties, labours and endeavours, but also the concerns of the poor, our nation, the world, peace and the family. With the mantra-like repetition of the 'Our Father', the ten 'Hail Marys' and the 'Glory be to the Father', we allow the Rosary to '"mark the rhythm of human life"', bringing it into harmony with the "rhythm" of God's own life, in the joyful communion of the Holy Trinity, our life's destiny and deepest longing', the source of all light.[87]

4

The Church Today

'Vatican Council II has invited us to contemplate the mystery of
the Church through biblical images which bring to light the reality
of the Church as a *communion* with its inseparable dimensions: the
communion of each Christian with Christ and the communion
of all Christians with one another.'

~ *Christifideles Laici*

The Church as Communion
'The most fundamental dimension of the Church'

The founder of the Focolare Movement, Chiara Lubich, often told of how during a lunchtime conversation with Pope John Paul, she had put to him the idea that in the future the president of the new movement should always be a woman, even though bishops, priests and men belonging to religious orders would be part of it. The Pope warmly supported this idea and eventually this became an element of the movement's statutes. In the course of his reply, however, he explained to her a vision of the Church that had been proposed by the Swiss theologian Hans Urs von Balthasar, and that he had clearly made his own in light of the ecclesiology of communion of the Second Vatican Council.

Taking the Gospel as his starting point, and reading it in a spiritual, contemplative manner, von Balthasar had proposed that just as Jesus was surrounded by various significant people during his life, so too the Risen Lord – who wills to be present in his Church to the end of time – cannot be isolated from the constellation of his historical life. Through the power of the Holy Spirit, the faith experiences of Mary, John the Baptist, the 'Twelve', the sisters of Bethany and Paul all flow into the Church as fundamental dimensions or profiles of the Church. The Church is made up, in other words, of many interacting profiles – hierarchical office (Peter); contemplative love (the Beloved Disciple); martyrdom (John the Baptist); concrete works of healing, teaching, and evangelising (the Sisters of Bethany); charismatic new beginnings (Paul) and focus on tradition (James).

It is clear why von Balthasar's personalist ecclesiology would have appealed to John Paul II, who was so rooted in Christian personalism. For the Pope, the focus was not so much on the Church as an objective institution but rather as an organic communion of many gifts and ministries. He brought out the communitarian side of the Church as the Mystical Body of Christ and People of God. Commenting on this, the American theologian and cardinal, Avery Dulles, wrote that:

John Paul II's favourite category for ecclesiology would
seem to be that of communion ... but he expounds it
in such a way that takes cognisance of the merits of
other approaches, such as those depicting the Church
as institution, sacrament, herald and servant. As a
personalist, Wojtyła clearly subordinates the institutional
and the external to the communal and the spiritual.[88]

In his apostolic exhortation on the laity, *Christifideles Laici*, Pope John
Paul focuses on the notion of Church as communion. The members
of the Church are bound in communion with one another not merely
sociologically or psychologically, but rather by spiritual bonds that bring
them into a supernatural relationship in their reciprocal membership in
the Body of Christ:

Ecclesial communion is more precisely likened to an
'organic' communion, analogous to that of a living and
functioning body. In fact, at one and the same time it
is characterised by a diversity and a complementarity
of vocations and states in life, of ministries, of charisms
and responsibilities. Because of this diversity and
complementarity every member of the lay faithful is seen
in relation to the whole body and offers a *totally unique
contribution* on behalf of the whole body.[89]

Very much influenced by the Council, John Paul points to the Trinity,
the divine communion of persons who love one another, as the supreme
model for the Church. The Church is, as the Second Vatican Council
put it, 'a people made one with the unity of the Father, the Son and the
Holy Spirit'.[90] The Church is like a family whose mutual love originates
in the Trinity and is poured into our hearts by the Holy Spirit. In
another document, the Pope emphasises the personal relationships that
should exist at every level of Church life and invites all to 'live the life
of the Trinity'.[91] In terms of the college of bishops, he spoke often of the
need for both 'effective' and 'affective' collegiality.

Taking up von Balthasar's notion of the many and various profiles
that co-exist in the Church, Pope John Paul makes an important
statement when he recalls that the Petrine dimension is essential

and fundamental to the life of the Church – that is, the sacramental-hierarchical means that build up the Church. The Crucified and Risen Christ works objectively through the Word preached, the sacraments (especially the Eucharist) and the ministry and charisms to build up the Church – but our response to these gifts is vital. As Bishop Klaus Hemmerle put it some years ago, 'what comes from above needs to be born from below'.[92] The sacramental-hierarchical gifts are means of grace, but the life that comes through them needs to be lived out in everyday personal and social existence. We must remember the goal – to be Jesus Christ, the Church, in the world. Pope John Paul calls this fundamental aspect 'the Marian profile' of the Church.

Mary, the first disciple, lets the Christ event become history in her and among us. That fundamental 'yes' still resides at the heart of the Church. Together, each one of us is called to echo that 'yes' so that the Church will radiate the presence of Jesus Christ in us and among us. It is the 'yes' of the Gospel lived, the 'yes' of holiness. The Marian dimension is about how the Christ event can be a transforming influence in our own lives and in the world around us.

In John Paul II's understanding, the deepest contents of renewal desired by the Second Vatican Council are to be found in the Marian dimension of the Church. In his view of things, the Marian principle was very much linked with the emerging lay face of the Church. It has to do with a renewed understanding of the role of women in the Church, as well as spirituality, dialogue and charisms. Above all, it has to do with the holiness that is essential for the mission of the Church today. Accordingly, speaking with the members of the Curia, Pope John Paul pointed out that 'the Marian profile is perhaps the most fundamental dimension of the Church – even more than the apostolic, Petrine profile to which it is profoundly united'.[93]

Crises in the Church
'An epochal dark night'

Having lived under communism and travelled around Europe, and as a man of profound reflection, before becoming Pope, Karol Wojtyła had already begun to realise that the crisis the Catholic Church was going through was not simply to be resolved by band-aid solutions. He went to the root of the problem and did not shirk the painful reality of what he observed there.

On the one hand, modern Western culture has seen huge strides forward in science, technology and wealth. The rights and values of freedom and equality are highly valued. There is a new take on the world. And yet, wealth hasn't always led to equity; nations still fight one another. More seriously, the optimism in progress at all costs has led to a loss of a sense of God, who remains beyond our grasp and control. In our times, faith is often discredited. There is suspicion about God. Human power and the dynamic of history itself have become absolute, with the result that 'despite all that they claim for themselves and all that is available to them, men and women of today are tempted by doubt concerning the meaning of life, tempted by anguish and nihilism'.[94]

The Church is not immune from the trials that men and women of Western culture are going through. The Church is no sealed train travelling through history. And so Pope John Paul II, speaking to the fifth Symposium of the Bishops of Europe on 5 October 1982, observed:

> ... these tests, these temptations and this outcome of
> the European drama not only questions Christianity and
> the Church from outside as a difficulty or an external
> obstacle to be overcome in the work of evangelisation ...
> but in a true sense they are interior to Christianity and
> the Church ...

The crises of European culture (and by extension Western culture) were, for John Paul II, not simply external events happening somewhere out there – beyond the Church – but the very crises of Christian culture itself. He pointed out that these crises, in particular the crisis in belief, arise especially in the European continent – the very place where Christianity first took root and became inculturated in everyday life. His reading, therefore, is that the crises experienced in Western culture are actually linked to a profound question of what it means to say we relate to God in Jesus Christ. The Christian claim that God revealed himself in his Son, Jesus Christ, took root in Europe. We've journeyed two thousand years within this understanding of God. Now that European and Western culture is going through various temptations, infidelities and risks regarding its belief in God, what we are actually seeing presented to us are the temptations, infidelities and risks that are at the core of humanity's relationship with God in Christ.[95] For John Paul this is not all negative. On the contrary, it could lead to a new and deeper penetration of the Christian vision of God and humanity. Have we really thought through the social and cultural implications of the fact that Jesus is divine-human? Indeed, the many thorny issues of our time – such as freedom and self-realisation, autonomy, inter-subjectivity and multiculturalism – all demand a deeper encounter with the God of Jesus Christ and a deeper understanding of what it means to be human in relation to this God.

Pope John Paul threw further light on what he meant by pointing to the mystical experience of the saint that he studied for his doctoral thesis – St John of the Cross. Taking up the Spanish mystic's thought about a 'dark night' of the senses and the soul, John Paul compares the cultural crisis we are going through in the Western world with that experienced in the spiritual life. Having started with enthusiasm and great light, it often happens that a person who is eagerly undertaking a spiritual journey undergoes a period of darkness where his or her faith is deepened and matures. The crisis of faith in the Western world today is something like such a dark night in one's personal journey, except that now it has acquired an epochal dimension of collective proportions and it is a whole continent or culture that is going through this trial.[96]

So yes, there are crises and there is darkness. But, in view of the analogy of the dark night that leads to new union with God, so too can the epochal collective dark night of today's Western culture, in Pope

John Paul II's view, be seen as the prelude to a new dawn – a new and profound experience and understanding of the God who has revealed himself eschatologically in Jesus Christ and who wants to live among us.[97]

Clerical Child Sexual Abuse
'To the victims and their families ... I express my profound concern'

On 23 April 2002, in the light of the crisis of child sexual abuse by clerics that injured so many and rocked the Church, Pope John Paul II summoned the American cardinals to Rome to discuss the issue. He told them, 'Like you, I too have been deeply grieved by the fact that priests and religious, whose vocation it is to help people live holy lives in the sight of God, have themselves caused such suffering and scandal to the young'.[98] Earlier, in 1999, in an address to the Bishops of Ireland, he spoke of his concern for the victims of sexual abuse on the part of clerics or religious: 'We must also pray that those who have been guilty of this wrong will recognise the evil nature of their actions and seek forgiveness.'

The sheer scale of the problem shocked many. In 2001, Pope John Paul had issued a *motu proprio* (a document on a specific topic issued on the Pope's initiative) entitled *Sacramentorum Sanctitatis Tutela*, aimed at clarifying what been left unclear since the publication of the 1983 Code of Canon Law: namely, that cases of clerical paedophilia should come under the competency of the Congregation for the Doctrine of the Faith. Sometimes it is said that the document was intended to prevent information being passed on to the civil authorities. The document didn't address that issue at all. The intention, rather, was to ensure that cases should be expedited swiftly and in a consistent manner throughout the world. In fact, the document was a watershed moment in the Vatican's dealing with the issue. John Paul II's address to the American cardinals in April 2002 was robust. He made clear that in any response to the issue, the victims had to have priority:

> The abuse which has caused this crisis is by every standard wrong and rightly considered a crime by society; it is also an appalling sin in the eyes of God. To the victims and their families, wherever they may be, I express my profound sense of solidarity and concern.

He understood the abuse of the young was a grave symptom of a deep crisis that called for purification, holiness and healing. He also believed that if the Church could address the problem of abuse with clarity and determination, it would be carrying out a service not only internally but for the wider community. However, he recognised that 'because of the great harm done by some priests and religious, the Church herself is viewed with distrust, and many are offended at the way in which the Church's leaders are perceived to have acted in this matter'. So he continued:

> It must be absolutely clear to the Catholic faithful, and to the wider community, that bishops and superiors are concerned, above all else, with the spiritual good of souls. People need to know that there is no place in the priesthood and religious life for those who would harm the young. They must know that bishops and priests are totally committed to the fullness of Catholic truth on matters of sexual morality, a truth as essential to the renewal of the priesthood and the episcopate as it is to the renewal of marriage and family life.

While knowing the bishops were now working to establish more reliable criteria to ensure that such terrible failures are not repeated, the Pope prayed that they would respond to the crisis with a genuine and effective pastoral charity for the victims, as well as for the priests and the entire Catholic community.

No doubt some could comment that, judged by today's standards, John Paul could have done more regarding the issue of clerical child abuse. He was himself aware of his limits in exercising the governing side of his ministry. His decisions, as well as his assessments of some individuals and situations, are open to question. As George Weigel comments: 'thus the life of John Paul II, for all its accomplishment and despite the richness of his spiritual life, demonstrates the ancient truth that no pope exercises infallible prudential judgment about men and circumstances' as distinct from matters of faith and morals.[99] But for all that, Pope John Paul II saw the issue of clerical child sexual abuse as a time of trial, pain and sorrow that would also bring a purification of the entire Catholic community.

The Lay Faithful
'You go into my vineyard too'

George Weigel once described John Paul II as a clergyman with a 'lay soul'.[100] Indeed, there can be no doubt he had a particular sensitivity to the lay vocation. Early on in life he was struck by the example of Jan Leopold Tyranowski, a clerk who had chosen to work in his father's tailor shop because such work would make it easier for him to develop his interior life. He was a man of especially deep spirituality. The Salesian priests had given him the task of creating a network of contacts with young people through what was called the 'Living Rosary' movement. Tyranowski concerned himself with the spiritual formation of the young people whom he met. His own spiritual formation was based on the writings of St John of the Cross and St Teresa of Avila and he helped the young Wojtyła to read their works.[101]

In 1988, Pope John Paul dedicated an apostolic exhortation to the theme of laity, *Christifideles Laici*. He also gave twenty-six talks on the laity in general audiences between 5 October 1993 and 21 September 1994. The lay vocation is rooted in baptism which brings all the baptised into a participation in the threefold office of Jesus Christ: prophet, priest and king/shepherd. Above all, the lay faithful express this participation in the temporal realm. Baptism launches the baptised into lives of working towards renewing all things in Christ, working, suffering and praying for the world, and bearing witness to the Gospel by word and deed.

For John Paul, the universal call to holiness was fundamental – holiness understood as the perfection of love. Laity live out this holiness in their family and social lives as well as their workplace. Nevertheless, it was clear that Pope John Paul also had the vast range of social, cultural and political arenas in mind. Laity are called to make the Gospel come alive in the worlds of media and politics, economics and medicine, science and culture, sports and recreation, education and health. In doing so they become salt of the earth, light of the world.

For lay people to become holy does not involve having to retreat to a monastery – it involves doing ordinary things extraordinarily well in one's everyday professional and social life.

John Paul presented a dynamic vision of how laity, religious and priests interrelate. As he puts it, 'They all share in a deeply basic meaning: that of ... *living out the commonly shared Christian dignity and the universal call to holiness in the perfection of love.*' He recognises that 'they are *different yet complementary*', and goes on to explain that we must always consider laity, religious and priests as, 'related to one another and serving each other.'[102]

Clearly, the fact that lay Christians are characterised, above all, by the secular character of their witness does not preclude them from participating in various ministries directly at the service of the inner life of the Church. With regard to lay ministry, John Paul notes, however, the risk of 'clericalising' the lay faithful. He does not deny lay ministries. His concern is to keep the focus on the overall lay profile of the Church – the whole purpose of the Church is not to be concerned only with its own inner life but to continue Jesus' mission of uniting the *whole* of humankind with God and with one another.

Priesthood and Consecrated Life
'Be a gift of yourself at the service of others'

When Pope John Paul II's pontificate was inaugurated in 1978, the decline in the number of ordinations to the priesthood and religious life was a cause of concern to many in the Church. Encouraging priests and religious, as well as vocations, to the priesthood and consecrated life became a priority for him.

A synod in 1990, dedicated to the theme of the formation of priests, resulted in the 1992 apostolic letter, *Pastores Dabo Vobis*. Each Holy Thursday John Paul wrote a letter to 'brother priests' on themes to do with the priesthood, but above all, it was his own witness that spoke. George Weigel quotes Cardinal William Baum as saying the Pope was 'the best vocation director the Church has ever had'.[103] It was his clarity that the priesthood is a vocation, a 'gift and mystery' and not merely a function, that attracted many. He showed how the gift of celibacy, far from repressing a man's heart, or depriving him of a family, expands it in love so that he can build up the wider family of the people of God.

John Paul thought of the priestly vocation in terms of the mystery of a 'wondrous exchange':

> A man offers his humanity to Christ, so that Christ may
> use him as an instrument of salvation, making him as it
> were into another Christ. Unless we grasp the mystery of
> this 'exchange', we will not understand how it can be that
> a young man, hearing the words 'Follow me!', can give up
> everything for Christ, in the certainty that if he follows
> this path he will find complete personal fulfilment.[104]

In a summary of a priest's identity, he commented in *Pastores Dabo Vobis*:

> In the Church and on behalf of the Church, priests are
> a sacramental representation of Jesus Christ – the head
> and shepherd – authoritatively proclaiming his word,
> repeating his acts of forgiveness and his offer of salvation
> – particularly in baptism, penance and the Eucharist,

showing his loving concern to the point of a total gift of
self for the flock, which they gather into unity and lead
to the Father through Christ and in the Spirit. In a word,
priests exist and act in order to proclaim the Gospel to the
world and to build up the Church in the name and person
of Christ the head and shepherd.[105]

John Paul presents the priest as a man 'for others', immersed in a 'rich
interconnection of relationships', placed in a sacramental way in communion with the bishop and other priests in order to serve the People of
God and the Church, and so draw everyone to Christ according to the
Lord's prayer: 'may they all be one, as we are one'.[106] In celebrating Mass
every day, the priest is renewed in his identity that is so strongly linked
with the Eucharist. For John Paul, it was clearly essential that priests root
their lives in prayer: 'Prayer makes the priest and through prayer the priest
becomes himself'.[107]

In his apostolic exhortation, *Vita Consecrata*, Pope John Paul spoke
of consecrated men and women who take vows of poverty, chastity and
obedience as being '*at the very heart of the Church*'.[108] In putting their lives
completely at the service of the Kingdom of God, they live the very way
of life that Jesus himself lived on earth. Recalling the continuous presence
of consecrated men and women in the Church throughout its history,
John Paul believed that in our world, where it often seems that the signs
of God's presence have been lost from sight, a convincing prophetic
witness – as provided by consecrated persons – is even more necessary. In
the Church they remind us of the fundamental values and beauty of the
Gospel and its radicality.

The exhortation is a rich biblical and theological meditation well
worth reading. Among other things, Pope John Paul underlined the need
for a creative fidelity to the founding charism and the subsequent spiritual
heritage of each institute:

> … it is precisely in this fidelity to the inspiration of the
> founders and foundresses, an inspiration which is itself a
> gift of the Holy Spirit, that the essential elements of the
> consecrated life can be more readily discerned and more
> fervently put into practice. (36)

The community life of religious orders is not to be underestimated because 'fraternal life, understood as a life shared in love, is an eloquent sign of ecclesial communion', and the community living in religious institutes and societies 'acquires special significance' (42). Indeed, religious life 'continues the mission of Christ with ... *fraternal life in community for the sake of the mission*' (72).

Certainly, consecrated women and men have contributed enormously to the Church and to humanity in terms of a huge variety of apostolic works and human development, serving the poorest and those most in need. Above all, however:

> ... more than in external works, the mission consists in making Christ present to the world through personal witness. This is the challenge, this is the primary task of the consecrated life! The more consecrated persons allow themselves to be conformed to Christ, the more Christ is made present and active in the world for the salvation of all. Thus it can be said that consecrated persons are 'in mission' by virtue of their very consecration. (72)

In short, the women and men in consecrated life mirror Christ, who himself lived a life totally directed to the Father and at the same time totally in missionary outreach to his brothers and sisters. They are signs for all in the Church of the eschatological fulfilment towards which the whole Church is tending; they anticipate it in their life of love of the neighbour 'to the end' (Jn 13:1).

The New Evangelisation
'Woe to me if I do not preach the Gospel!'

It has often been noted that Pope John Paul is the person who is said to have met more people than anyone before him. There was a drive in him to go out to people and evangelise, but he knew the classical means of doing so weren't enough. Something more was needed. In 1983, in an often-cited speech to the Bishops of South America, he coined the expression 'new evangelisation' explaining it is 'one that is new in its ardour, new in its methods, and new in its means of expression.'[109]

There can be no doubt that he saw evangelisation as a priority for the Church. He was realistic enough to recognise that in countries evangelised many centuries ago, the reality of a 'Christian society' – that is, a society that takes the Gospel values as its explicit measure – is now gone. In 2001, he commented:

> Today we must courageously face a situation which is becoming increasingly diversified and demanding, in the context of 'globalization' and of the consequent new and uncertain mingling of peoples and cultures. Over the years, I have often repeated the summons to the *new evangelisation*. I do so again now, especially in order to insist that we must rekindle in ourselves the impetus of the beginnings and allow ourselves to be filled with the ardour of the apostolic preaching which followed Pentecost. We must revive in ourselves the burning conviction of Paul, who cried out: 'Woe to me if I do not preach the Gospel' (1 Cor 9:16).[110]

John Paul's own ministry spoke of this new ardour, method and expression: the World Youth Days became platforms for reaching young people, he looked to new ecclesial communities and movements for experiences that can speak to people today and no other Pope has engaged the media so powerfully in communicating the Gospel. In an apostolic letter, *The Rapid Development* in January 2005, he wrote: 'Do not be afraid of new technologies! These rank "among the marvellous things" ... which God has placed at our disposal in order to discover, use and make known the truth.'[111] He was so aware that 'The communications media have acquired such importance as to be the principal means of guidance and inspiration for many people in their personal, familial and social behaviour.'[112]

Above all, however, John Paul knew that what was needed most in our times was a new encounter with the person of Jesus Christ. We need new ways and platforms for people to cross paths with Jesus Christ. As he put it in the 2001 letter, 'the men and women of our own day – often perhaps unconsciously – ask believers not only to "speak" of Christ, but in a certain sense to "show" him to them.'[113] His own life, with its measureless love for the neighbour, embodied his point. In his case, the messenger clearly was the message! He showed us how important it is 'to be' the message of love and 'to speak' of it. Evangelisation, for John Paul, was always joyful and to be carried out 'with the greatest respect.'[114]

The New Ecclesial Movements and Communities
'You are this providential response to the critical challenge'

It would be difficult to exaggerate the role of Pope John Paul II in encouraging new movements and communities in the life of the Church. In numerous audiences and meetings, letters, visits and lunches, he built up vibrant relationships with the founders, leaders and members of the new movements. For him they were clearly linked with reception of the Second Vatican Council and the 'new Pentecost' wished for by Pope John XXIII. So, from the beginning of his pontificate he made a point of meeting with movements:

> I followed their work attentively, accompanying them with prayer and constant encouragement. From the beginning of my pontificate, I have given special importance to the progress of ecclesial movements, and I have had the opportunity to appreciate the results of their widespread and growing presence during my pastoral visits to parishes and my apostolic journeys ... I have been able to point to them as something new that is still waiting to be properly accepted and appreciated.[115]

Just a decade after the 1987 Synod on the Laity, a very significant gathering of over 300,000 members of movements and ecclesial communities took place in St Peter's Square. This iconic gathering, on 31 May 1998, has been described by Cardinal Ryłko, the current president of the Pontifical Council for the Laity, as a 'decisive turning point for the life and mission of movements and communities.'[116] Among the founders of the new movements who offered their testimonies to the Pope and spoke to the packed Square were Chiara Lubich of the Focolare, Monsignor Luigi Giussani of Communion and Liberation, Kiko Argüello of the Neocatechumenate Way, Jean Vanier of L'Arche and Charles Whitehead of Charismatic Renewal.

The event was 'truly unprecedented' and, in his address, the Pope explained how he understood the new movements as an expression of the Church's charismatic or prophetic dimension that was rediscovered at the Second Vatican Council: 'The institutional and charismatic aspects are co-essential as it were to the Church's constitution. They contribute, although differently, to the life, renewal and sanctification of God's People.'[117]

Pope John Paul also proposed that 'a new stage' was now unfolding for the movements: that of ecclesial maturity. He invited them to embark upon a journey of bearing more 'mature' fruits of communion and commitment which 'the Church expects from you'. He explained his own passionate commitment to proposing movements:

> In our world, often dominated by a secularized culture which encourages and promotes models of life without God, the faith of many is sorely tested, and is frequently stifled and dies. Thus we see an urgent need for powerful proclamation and solid, in-depth Christian formation. There is so much need today for mature Christian personalities, conscious of their baptismal identity, of their vocation and mission in the Church and in the world! There is great need for living Christian communities! And here are the movements and the new ecclesial communities: they are the response, given by the Holy Spirit, to this critical challenge at the end of the millennium. You are this providential response. (7)

The Pope listed aspects he had observed in the movements. They have helped people rediscover their baptism, appreciate the gifts of the Spirit, gain a new trust in the sacrament of reconciliation and recognise the Eucharist as the source and summit of all Christian life. Thanks to their involvement in movements, families have been helped to become true 'domestic churches'. Vocations to ministerial priesthood and religious life and new forms of lay life inspired by the evangelical counsels, have also been fostered by movements.

Reminding the movements of the role of discernment that the competent ecclesiastical authorities have, he concluded with a rousing mandate:

Today, from this upper room in St Peter's Square, a great prayer rises: Come, Holy Spirit, come and renew the face of the earth ... Come, Holy Spirit, and make ever more fruitful the charisms that you have bestowed on us ... Today from this square, Christ says to each of you: 'Go into all the world and preach the gospel to the whole creation' (Mk 16:15). He is counting on every one of you, and so is the Church. 'Lo', the Lord promises, 'I am with you always to the close of the age' (Mt 28:20). (9)

5

A Pilgrim of Dialogue

'As we open ourselves in dialogue to one another,
we also open ourselves to God.'

~ *To Representatives of Various Religions of India*
Madras, 5 February 1986

Dialogue and Solidarity
'A Pope for all peoples'

When he first became Pope, people wondered if John Paul II would continue Pope Paul VI's openness to dialogue. But in April 1979, when he met the members of the then Secretariat for Non-Christians, he assured them he would. Looking back over his long pontificate it can certainly be said that John Paul II truly became a pilgrim of dialogue. Pilgrims set out along the journey aware of the goal, but not sure of the road along which they are going to travel. They don't know the difficulties that are going to crop up. And they have no idea of who their travelling companions will be. They only get to know them along the way and with them they face the unforeseen storms and difficulties, as well as the joy of discoveries, sharing and fraternity. All of this resonates with the life and ministry of Pope John Paul – if there is an abiding image of him, it is that of a world pilgrim! In 2000, the *Economist* magazine called him a 'A pope for all peoples.'[118]

It would be impossible to calculate just how many personal meetings he had with heads of state and government, academics, leaders of society and peoples worldwide to encourage a culture of dialogue, peace and fraternity in the course of more than 103 international journeys. He spoke in assemblies such as the UN in New York, UNESCO in Paris, FAO in Rome, as well as the various international bodies in Geneva and Strasbourg.

For John Paul II, diversity was not something to be afraid of. On the contrary – he considered it a launching pad towards a dialogue that builds up the human family:

> When 'diversities' converge and are integrated they start a 'friendly coexistence of differences'. Values are rediscovered that are common to every culture, which unite rather than divide and have put down roots in the same human soil. This encourages the development of a fruitful dialogue in order to prepare a path to reciprocal tolerance, realistic and respectful of the particularities of each one.[119]

He promoted dialogue at every chance. Eighty-two new apostolic nunciatures were opened during his long pontificate, bringing the number of states with which the Holy See has official relations to 174. John Paul wanted the nunciatures to be homes of international dialogue. The Pontifical Council for Justice and Peace was dedicated to promoting the Church's social doctrine and activity, particularly in relation to the vision of the world as a family of peoples at peace with one another.

In his first encyclical, *Redemptor Hominis*, John Paul took up the notion of the Church's 'circles' of dialogue that Pope Paul VI had outlined: with all people of goodwill, with members of other religions, with other churches and ecclesial communities and within the Church itself. In his 1986 Message for the World Day of Peace he called for dialogue with no frontiers:

> The right path to a world community in which justice and peace will reign without frontiers ... is *the path of solidarity, dialogue and universal brotherhood*. This is the only path possible. Political, economic, social and cultural relations and systems must be imbued with the values of solidarity and dialogue which, in turn, require an *institutional dimension* in the form of special organisms of the world community that will watch over the common good of all peoples.[120]

Dialogue and solidarity are the means by which people discover one another and discover the good hopes and peaceful aspirations that too often lie hidden in their hearts. He indicates what is to be gained from adopting a spirit of solidarity and dialogue: respect for every human person and respect for the true values and cultures of others – respect for the legitimate autonomy and self-determination of others.

Such dialogue will prompt us to look beyond ourselves in order to understand and support the good of others, contribute our own resources in social solidarity for the development and growth that come from equity and justice and build the structures that will ensure that social solidarity and dialogue are permanent features of the world we live in.

Difficulties can arise, however. That is where perseverance comes in. Christians need to recall that they are animated by a lively hope, capable of hoping against hope (cf. Rom 4:18): 'To all of you who believe in God I appeal that you live your lives in the awareness of being one family under the fatherhood of God.'[121]

Ecumenism
'To believe in Christ means to desire unity'

When the bishops of Poland came to the Second Vatican Council, they were among those who wanted ecumenism to be a central theme. However John Paul II became the Bishop of Rome just as ecumenism was moving from a flush of enthusiasm after Vatican II into a new moment of transition, searching and difficulties. Sometimes he was criticised for what many considered a slowing down in ecumenism. Yet, his sense of its value was strong. Cardinal Kasper, who came from Germany in the 1990s to head up the Pontifical Council for Promoting Christian Unity, is on record as stating his surprise at just how fervently the Pope considered ecumenism as one of his priorities.

In his Last Will and Testament John Paul specifically mentions the opening of the Holy Door of the Basilica of St Paul Outside the Walls during the Jubilee Year 2000. Photographs of this event show the Pope kneeling at the door with the Anglican Archbishop of Canterbury, Dr Carey, on one side, and the Orthodox bishop Metropolitan Athanasius of Heliopolis, on the other. This image, wrote John Paul, 'remained imprinted in my memory in a particular way'. The photographs of the event are like an icon (although it seems it hadn't been planned that way), revealing more than words could about the spirituality, fraternal love, humility and prayer that John Paul II believed to be at the heart of any healthy ecumenism.

John Paul's vision of ecumenism sprang from the Council. In November 2004, the ailing Pontiff attended Vespers celebrated by a gathering of official ecumenical delegates to mark the fortieth anniversary of the Council's major document on ecumenism, *Unitatis Redintegratio* (*The Restoration of Unity*). It was touching to see him being taken through St Peter's Basilica in a wheelchair. He wanted to reaffirm that the Catholic Church is irrevocably committed to ecumenism:

> We no longer consider other Christians as distant or strangers, but see them as brothers and sisters ... We are grateful to God to see that in recent years many of the

faithful across the world have been moved by an ardent desire for the unity of all Christians. I warmly thank those who have made themselves instruments of the Spirit and have worked and prayed for this process of rapprochement and reconciliation.[122]

In his 1994 book, *Crossing the Threshold of Hope*, John Paul wrote of the divisions in Christianity. Like any of us, he asks the questions: how did God allow it happen? What purpose does it serve? He gives a courageous answer when he says that as well as the limits and sinfulness of people at the time of the Reformation, the divisions were possibly permitted by God as 'a path continually leading the Church to discover the untold wealth contained in Christ's Gospel'. He further comments that 'perhaps all this wealth would not have come to light otherwise' and concludes that 'It is necessary for humanity to achieve unity through plurality, to learn how to come together in the one Church, even while presenting a plurality of ways of thinking and acting, of cultures and civilization.'[123]

In other words, there are all kinds of treasures in the Gospel that need to be discovered. Perhaps the pain of separation has its silver lining in that different aspects of the Gospel have been highlighted by various church traditions. The rupture of unity leads eventually to the rebuilding of relationships, but this time enriched in a communion where everyone defines themselves not in opposition to, but rather in relation to the others, as well as in relation to the common source that unites them. This is the paradox of ecumenism. It is in losing that we find. Together each one contributes to the deeper experience of the 'Catholic', in the sense of the 'whole' faith.

In his encyclical on unity, *Ut Unum Sint* (*May They All Be One*) – seen by many as having relaunched the ecumenical movement in the 1990s – Pope John Paul summarised the dynamic of Christian unity in a sentence that's worth meditating:

> To believe in Christ means to desire unity; to desire unity means to desire the Church; to desire the Church means to desire the communion of grace which corresponds to the Father's plan from all eternity. Such is the meaning of Christ's prayer: "*Ut unum sint*".[124]

Very early in his pontificate, John Paul visited Constantinople and initiated the Catholic–Orthodox dialogue. He was convinced that reconciliation between Eastern and Western Christianity would move the whole ecumenical movement along, enabling the Church 'to breathe with both lungs', as he often repeated. In an address to the Secretariat for Christian Unity in 1980 he commented:

> I am convinced that a re-articulation of the ancient Eastern and Western traditions and the balancing exchange that will result when full communion is found again, may be of great importance to heal the divisions that came about in the West in the sixteenth century.[125]

In proposing spiritual ecumenism at the heart of the ecumenical venture, John Paul recognised the need for a dialogue of conversion of all involved. Ecumenism can't simply be a politics based on negotiating skills and compromise tactics. Rather it requires sincerely listening to one another, understanding each other, living for others, striving for holiness, purifying the memory of past mistakes and forgiving past errors. John Paul describes the profound dimension of dialogue when he writes that through it we are entering 'that interior space where Christ, the source of the Church's unity, can effectively act, with all the power of his Spirit, the Paraclete'.[126] For this to happen, we need to live out a spirituality of communion and fellowship together.

A striking feature of *Ut Unum Sint* was Pope John Paul's readiness to review the exercise of the ministry of the Pope. Obviously, it was not a question of altering the meaning of the ministry that Jesus had in mind when he made Peter the 'rock' of the Church, but John Paul recognised the need to review, in the light of the Gospel, the historical form with which it is carried out concretely. During the gathering of the world's religious leaders in Assisi in 1986, the Christian leaders discovered in a new way that what unites them is more than what divides them. Afterwards, Robert Runcie, the then Archbishop of Canterbury, commented:

> In Assisi we saw that the Bishop of Rome could gather the Christian churches together ... Could not all Christians come to reconsider the kind of primacy that the Bishop

of Rome exercised within the early Church, a 'presiding in love' for the sake of the unity of the churches in the diversity of their mission.[127]

Pope John Paul continued in his ecumenical relations to the end. On 7 May 2000, during the Jubilee Year, he celebrated the twentieth-century martyrs who form 'a common inheritance of Catholics, Orthodox, Anglicans and Protestants'. As he put it: 'the ecumenism of the martyrs and the witnesses to the faith is the most convincing of all ... it shows the path to unity'.[128] In 2004, he gave the relics of the saints Gregory of Nanzianzen and John Chrysostom to the Ecumenical Patriarch of Constantinople, Bartholomew I – signifying the desire of the Church of East and West to journey together and 'to breathe with two lungs'.

Interreligious Dialogue
'Treat others as you would like others to treat you'

The media has brought us so many images of the Pope meeting with Jews and Muslims, Buddhists and Hindus that it's easy to recall his commitment to interreligious dialogue, which opened up for the Catholic Church with the Second Vatican Council's milestone document, *Nostra Aetate*.

In 1985, invited by King Hassan, John Paul met and spoke with forty thousand young Muslims in Casablanca, Morocco. And who could forget his trip to the Holy Land in 2000? In a veritable tour de force the Pope moved from the Palestinian refugee camp of Deheisheh to the Yad Vashem Mausoleum, from the Mosques to the Temple and the Western Wall. In some ways, however, it was the great Assisi meeting of world religious leaders coming together to pray in 1986 that will remain as one of the masterpieces of his pontificate.

Pope John Paul spoke often of interreligious dialogue with members of the Curia, diplomats and bishops on their *ad limina* visits, as well as during general audiences on Wednesdays. He also reflected on this dialogue in official documents, such as the 1990 encyclical letter, *Redemptoris Missio*:

> A vast field lies open to dialogue, which can assume many forms and expressions: from exchanges between experts in religious traditions or official representatives of those traditions to cooperation for integral development and the safeguarding of religious values; and from a sharing of their respective spiritual experiences to the so-called 'dialogue of life', through which believers of different religions bear witness before each other in daily life to their own human and spiritual values, and help each other to live according to those values in order to build a more just and fraternal society. Each member of the faithful and all Christian communities are called to practice dialogue, although not always to the same degree or in the same way.[129]

We have already reviewed how John Paul II's commitment to inter-religious dialogue was based on his understanding of the Triune God's all-embracing plan for humanity. In particular, he was attentive to the role of the Spirit in the world: 'every authentic prayer is prompted by the Holy Spirit, who is mysteriously present in every human heart'. In Madras, India, he stated: 'as we open ourselves in dialogue to one another, we also open ourselves to God'.[130]

From early on in his pontificate, it was clear that Pope John Paul enjoyed a warm relationship with Jews, and his condemnation of anti-Semitism is well known. Indeed, his dialogue with Jews wasn't simply an instance of interreligious dialogue. It was much more: he considered the Jewish people as our 'elder brothers and sisters'.[131] On 13 April 1986, John Paul was the first Pope since Peter to enter the Synagogue of Rome.

From his earliest years in Poland, Karol Wojtyła had known many Jews and counted them among his friends. As Pope he often recalled his closeness to the Jewish community and he belonged to a generation for which relationships with Jews were a daily occurrence: a quarter of his classmates at elementary school were Jews, his friendship with school friend Jerzy Kluger lasted throughout his life, and Ginka Beer, a Jewish neighbour in Wadowice, recalls how 'there was only one family who never showed any racial hostility towards us, and that was Lolek and his dad'.[132] As a young priest, he refused to baptise a six-year-old boy named Hiller, after the woman who brought the child to him explained that his father was Jewish and that his mother had been killed by the Nazis in the Kraków ghetto. The young curate felt it would be disloyal to baptise the child as a Catholic and suggested he should be sent to his family in America. A month later the child was sent there.

John Paul emphasised that the covenant with the Jewish people – 'Abraham's stock' – was irrevocable. On that basis and recognising that 'our two religious communities are connected and closely related at the very level of their respective religious identities', Pope John Paul committed himself wholeheartedly to improving relations, recognising that 'as children of Abraham, we, Christians and Jews, are called to be a blessing to the world. In order to be such, we must be first a blessing to one another.'[133]

There were controversial moments, such as those surrounding the Auschwitz convent, Edith Stein's beatification, and the visit of Kurt Waldheim to the Vatican, but Pope John Paul kept going. He encouraged many forms of Catholic–Jewish dialogue and spearheaded the publication by the Commission for Religious Relations with the Jews of such documents as *Notes on the Correct Way to Present the Jews and Judaism in Preaching and Catechesis in the Roman Catholic Church* (1985) and *We Remember: A Reflection on the Shoah* (1998). In short, as Rabbi Jack Bemporad commented:

> No Pope in history had ever done more than John Paul II to further the development of Jewish–Christian relations. He was the first [Pope] to enter a synagogue, to push for and establish diplomatic relations with Israel, and always made sure he met with the leaders of Jewish communities in every country he visited.[134]

Pope John Paul II also fostered dialogue with Muslims. Meeting with the Muslim leaders at the Umayyad Great Mosque in Damascus in May 2001, he affirmed:

> It is important that Muslims and Christians continue to explore philosophical and theological questions together, in order to come to a more objective and comprehensive knowledge of each others' religious beliefs. Better mutual understanding will surely lead, at the practical level, to a new way of presenting our two religions not in opposition, as has happened too often in the past, but in partnership for the good of the human family.[135]

In his 1991 message to Muslims on the occasion of Eid-al-Fitr, John Paul concluded his greeting with the words of one of his predecessors, Pope Gregory VII, who wrote to Al-Nasir, the Muslim ruler of Bijaya (present-day Algeria) in 1076. In referring to the golden rule that is found in some form in all the world's religious texts – 'treat others as you would want them to treat you' – Pope Gregory had written:

> Almighty God, who wishes that all should be saved and none lost, approves of nothing in us so much as that after loving him one should love his fellow man, and that one should not do to others what one does not want done to

oneself. You and we owe this charity to ourselves especially because we believe in and confess one God, admittedly in a different way, and daily praise and venerate him, the Creator of the world and Ruler of this world.[136]

John Paul II's outreach deeply touched the members of other religions and a few days after his death, the *Osservatore Romano* newspaper carried a number of testimonies to him. Among them, was this from a young Palestinian Muslim woman named Fatima: 'The Pope belongs to everyone, also to me a Muslim. He belongs to everyone because he gave a voice to all, regardless of one's religion, with justice, love, peace, freedom and dignity.'

Science and Religion in Dialogue
'Truth cannot contradict Truth'

During a commemoration in 1979, marking the centennial of the birth of the great Jewish mathematician and physicist Albert Einstein, Pope John Paul proposed re-examining the case of Galileo Galilei. Since his first condemnation in 1633 for maintaining that the earth revolved around the sun, Galileo's name had become synonymous with the Church's negative attitude to science. This was disastrous for a Church that had previously promoted the sciences.

John Paul himself was fascinated by science since his time in Kraków, where he was friendly with a number of scientists, including nuclear physicists. From meetings and discussions throughout his life with experts in the natural sciences, physicists and biologists, he 'learned to appreciate the importance of those other branches of knowledge which involve the scientific disciplines' and to recognise that 'these are likewise capable of attaining the truth from different aspects'.[137] He was convinced that Galileo had suffered much at the hands of men and the organs of the church. So on 10 November 1979, in addressing the Pontifical Academy of Sciences, he said:

> I submit that theologians, men of science and historians, in a spirit of sincere collaboration, should deepen the examination of the Galileo case ... to honour the truth of the faith and of science and to open the door to their future collaboration.[138]

A special Galileo Commission was set up, which vindicated the scientist in a formal statement a year later. But this was only a first step in John Paul's initiatives in advocating a greater dialogical approach to the relationship between theology and the sciences of nature. The time for polemics was over. In an address to the Pontifical Academy of the Sciences on 23 October 1996, in relation to the evolutionary phenomenon and related theories, he reaffirmed the principle that 'truth cannot contradict, truth'. Scientific truth such as that of evolutionary human origins cannot contradict, and cannot be contradicted by, the revealed truth concerning the human person. He continued: 'Science can purify religion from error and superstition; religion can purify science from idolatry and false absolutes. Each one can help others enter into a wider world, a world in which both can prosper.'[139] Both science and theology can support and value the specific contribution of each other as distinct elements within our common human culture.

On the publication of the proceedings of a 'study week' promoted by Pope John Paul on the relationship between theology, philosophy and the natural sciences, he wrote a letter to Father George Coyne, the Jesuit astronomer, who was at the time the director of the Vatican Observatory in Castel Gandolfo:

> To be more specific, both religion and science must preserve their autonomy and their distinctiveness. Religion is not founded on science nor is science an extension of religion. Each should possess its own principles, its pattern of procedures, its diversities of interpretation and its own conclusions. Christianity possesses the source of its justification within itself and does not expect science to constitute its primary apologetic. Science must bear witness to its own worth. While each can and should support the other as distinct dimensions of a common human culture, neither ought to assume that it forms a necessary premise for the other. The unprecedented opportunity we have today is for a common interactive relationship in which each discipline retains its integrity and yet is radically open to the discoveries and insights of the other.[140]

Pope John Paul was hopeful that 'as dialogue and common searching continue, there will be growth towards mutual understanding and a gradual uncovering of common concerns which will provide the basis for further research and discussion.'[141]

Some scientists have warmly endorsed the positive comments made by John Paul on the interaction between science and religion. For instance, Stephen Jay Gould, probably the best known writer on evolution in the USA, commenting on John Paul's 1996 address, wrote:

I happily endorse this turn of events as gospel – literally good news. I represent the magisterium of science, but I welcome the support of a primary leader from the other major magisterium of our complex lives. And I recall the wisdom of King Solomon: 'As cold waters to a thirsty soul, so is good news from a far country' (Prov, 25:25).[142]

6

A Pastor For All

'Faith is strengthened when it is given to others.'

~ *Redemptoris Missio*

The Parish Community
'How I loved the visits to the parishes!'

In John Paul II's recollection of the journey to his first parish, you can almost hear him savouring both the excitement and sacred reverence:

> I went from Cracow to Gdów by bus, and from there
> a local man gave me a ride in his cart to the village of
> Marszowice; from there he advised me to take a shortcut
> through the fields on foot. I could already see the church
> of Niegowić in the distance. It was harvest time. I walked
> through the fields of grain with the crops in part already
> reaped, and in part still waving in the wind. When I finally
> reached the territory of Niegowić parish, I knelt down
> and kissed the ground. It was a gesture I had learned from
> St John Mary Vianney. In the Church I made a visit to
> the Blessed Sacrament and then introduced myself to the
> parish priest ... who welcomed me very cordially ... And so
> I began my pastoral work in my first parish.[143]

Since he saw the parish as the 'most immediate and visible expression' of the Church, the place where the Church is seen locally, 'living in the midst of the homes of her sons and daughters' then it is no surprise that he loved the many parish visits he undertook while Pope.[144] He managed to visit most of the parishes of the diocese of Rome. Speaking to the clergy of the diocese of Rome the first time he met them, he said:

> With regard to the parish, how profoundly true I find
> the affirmation that the bishop feels more at ease 'in
> the parish'! How I loved the visits to the parishes –
> fundamental organisational cells of the Church and at
> same time of the community of the People of God.[145]

To say the parish has passed, and is passing, through a critical period is an understatement. In previous times it was for many, especially in rural areas, the centre of social and religious life. However, with rapidly changing cultural and social circumstances, it has gradually become more of a 'service station' for religious functions. While clearly appreciating the continuing importance of the parish, John Paul was not afraid to ask the questions: in modern cities, is the parish up to the task of responding to the challenge of a world that is increasingly fragmented? Does it have enough life to ensure the Good News can impact on people – young, old, marginalised, disappointed or indifferent?

Pope John Paul described the vocation of the parish as being that of a 'family, fraternal and welcoming home, a fraternity animated by a spirit of unity, the family of God in a concrete place'. For him:

> ... the parish is not principally a structure, a territory, a building. The parish is firstly a community of the faithful ... This is the task of the parish today: to be a community, to rediscover itself as community. You are not Christians on your own. To be Christians means to believe and live one's faith with others, to be Church, community.[146]

John Paul encouraged collaboration between all those involved in diverse but complementary ministries and charisms. He encouraged the promotion of parish and pastoral councils. In their life of communion, the parish communities, in Pope John Paul's view, are called to be an anticipation of the civilisation of love:

> The world today, often far from God, looks more to deeds than to words. But it is Christ himself who launches us along this way: 'by this all will know you are my disciples if you have love for one another'. The parish is the privileged place to give this witness, repeating in our time the miracle of the first communities, the miracle of a new life that is not just spiritual but social and historical.[147]

As a young priest he recognised the need to be 'living' one's faith in order to communicate it. To a seminarian friend, Mieczysaw Maliñ, who came to visit him on several occasions, he spoke of the risk of becoming 'office-clerk' priests:

When we talk about confession ... you can't settle matters
with a smooth word. You have to establish a dialogue and
treat it seriously and from the heart ... So the question
is whether we can preserve the apostolic values. In the
absence of deep inner life, a priest will imperceptibly turn
into an office clerk, and his apostolate will turn into a
parish office routine, just solving daily problems.[148]

The missionary dimension of the parish was very much to the fore John
Paul's thought. The world is rapidly changing. So a new pastoral vision
is needed. This means going beyond the goals of simply preserving the
faith and caring for one's own parish community. It involves openness
to the wider diocesan reality, reference to the local bishop and making
links with neighbouring parishes, as well as openness to new charisms
and new ecclesial experiences.

The Family as the 'Church in miniature'
'The family is the first and most important path of the Church'

There's something of a paradox in the fact that a man who lost all his family members at a relatively young age should find himself in his later years becoming a champion of family values. But that is precisely what Pope John Paul did when the traditional institution of the family was collapsing in many parts of the world with, as he believed, devastating effects upon society.

One cannot help but be struck by his astuteness in pointing out what is so often missing in mainstream pastoral ministry: among the many ways the Church proceeds 'the family is the first and most important'.[149] Salvation isn't just about individuals.

Throughout his time as a young priest, bishop and cardinal, John Paul had always been attentive to families. In Kraków in 1960, he had set up a family institute with mother-of-four, Wanda Poltawska. As Pope, the very first synod of bishops he summoned and prepared was on family, leading to the 1981 apostolic letter dedicated to that theme, *Familiaris Consortio*. Before his pontificate there had simply been a Committee for the Family in the Vatican departments – John Paul expanded this to become a Pontifical Council for the Family. During the 1994 UN International Year of the Family, he was particularly active at the World Conference on Population and Development held in Cairo (at which the current Archbishop of Dublin, Diarmuid Martin represented the Holy See) in campaigning for the protection of family values. Moreover, he established multidisciplinary institutes for research into marriage and family, which can now be found in Rome, Washington and Melbourne, as well as in countries such as Brazil, India, Benin, Mexico and Spain.

In his 1994 *Letter to Families*, John Paul pointed out that each family is unique and that family plays a fundamental role in the development of each and every person. When it is lacking, a person will carry a burden in their lives. Emerging from families, we go forward to create new family units:

Even if someone chooses to remain single, the family
continues to be, as it were, his or her existential horizon,
that fundamental community in which the whole network
of social relations is grounded, from the closest and most
immediate to the most distant. Do we not often speak of
the 'human family' when referring to all the people living
in the world?[150]

While the family is experienced the world over, Pope John Paul grounds
his vision of it in nothing less than the divine community of the Trinity
– Three Persons who love one another. Jesus has revealed to us the
measure of love needed in all family relations: to be able to give your life
for one another. And when there are problems in families, again it is to
the Crucified and Risen Christ we can turn to find the way to live out
our situation.

Through the sacrament of marriage, the relationship of husband and
wife (and the other relationships within the family unit that come to life
through their union) takes on a new value – that of being a 'domestic
Church'.[151] In other words, the mutual love that originates in Christ
forms the members of the family into a 'Church in miniature'. It has,
therefore, a mission to reveal and communicate love. It becomes the
place where its members 'learn' to be with and for others.

However, marriages do break down and Pope John Paul was aware of
the pastoral issues regarding the divorced and re-married whose union
has not been annulled by the Church. He recognised the pain caused to
those involved in this situation, not least by the fact that they are unable
to receive the Eucharist. Nevertheless, he comments that the Church
must ensure that such persons 'do not consider themselves as separated
from the Church', and continues:

They should be encouraged to listen to the word of God,
to attend the Sacrifice of the Mass, to persevere in prayer,
to contribute to works of charity and to community
efforts in favour of justice, to bring up their children in
the Christian faith, to cultivate the spirit and practice of
penance and thus implore, day by day, God's grace.[152]

The *Letter to Children*
'Dear children ... The Pope counts very much on your prayers'

At Christmas time, during the 1994 Year of the Family, Pope John Paul wrote a letter to children. The Christmas setting lent warmth to the text as he conjured up images of his own early Christmases in Poland:

> I would hurry to the crib together with the other boys and girls to relive what happened 2000 years ago in Palestine. We children expressed our joy mostly in song. How beautiful and moving are the Christmas carols which in the tradition of every people are sung around the crib! What deep thoughts they contain, and above all what joy and tenderness they express about the Divine Child who came into the world that Holy Night![153]

However, the Pope was no sentimentalist. He also knew that many children in different parts of the world suffer and are threatened: many are victims of war, are abandoned by their parents and suffer 'forms of violence and arrogance from grown-ups' (1).

Above all, Pope John Paul's letter points to the child Jesus who, in his public ministry as an adult, would go on to '*show an extraordinary love for children*':

> He will say to the Apostles: 'Let the children come to me, do not hinder them', and he will add: 'for to such belongs the kingdom of God' (Mk 10:14). Another time, as the Apostles are arguing about who is the greatest, he will put a child in front of them and say: 'Unless you turn and become like children, you will never enter the kingdom of heaven' (Mt 18:3). On that occasion, he also spoke harsh words of warning: 'Whoever causes one of these little ones who believes in me to sin, it would be better for him to have a great millstone fastened round his neck and to be drowned in the depth of the sea' (Mt 18:6).

On this basis, Pope John Paul opens our eyes to 'How *important children are in the eyes of Jesus!* We could even say that *the Gospel is full of the truth about children.* The whole of the Gospel could actually be read as the "Gospel of children".'

Children can be seen as models for grown-ups in their relationship to God. What we see in them are attitudes such as simplicity, trust and purity. They show us how we need to be directed towards God as children of the one Father.

In the course of his letter, John Paul recalls the children in the history of the Church who have given profound example. He mentions boys and girls such as Agnes, Agatha and Tarcisius, who lived in the first centuries and are still known and venerated throughout the Church for their heroism. St Tarcisius is called the 'martyr of the Eucharist' because he preferred to die rather than give up Jesus, whom he was carrying under the appearance of bread. John Paul also refers us to St Bernadette of Lourdes, the children of La Salette, and to Lucia, Francisco and Jacinta of Fatima. It cannot be forgotten: children were often entrusted with important tasks for the life of the Church and of humanity.

In a poignant comment, Pope John Paul trusts in children, saying *'What enormous power the prayer of children has!'* Their way of praying becomes a model for all. They pray with simple and complete trust. And so John Paul declares, '*The Pope counts very much on your prayers*' and invites children to join him in prayer: 'We must pray together and pray hard, that humanity, made up of billions of human beings, may become more and more the family of God and able to live in peace.'

Young People
'You are the future of the world; you are the hope of the Church; you are my hope'

Some years ago a priest friend told me of a young married man in his parish who was dying. The man had been a lecturer at a third-level college. Though he hadn't always practiced his faith, he faced death with courage and peace, explaining to my priest friend: 'I am not afraid; after all, Pope John Paul II taught me to believe in eternal life.' He was referring to his participation in one of the first World Youth Days.

That John Paul enjoyed a particular friendship with young people is well known. Left orphaned himself at an early age, he had developed many profound friendships with his young friends at the theatre, then at work and in the seminary. As a priest he dedicated himself especially to the young and was affectionately known to them as 'uncle'. He believed in young people and trusted them. And so he could sincerely say to them, as he did on the very day of the inauguration of his papal ministry at the conclusion of the liturgy, 'You are the hope of the church and of the world. You are my hope.'[154] His spontaneous declaration, 'Young People, I love you!' (for example, at the Youth Mass in Galway), often prompted the warm response: 'John Paul II, we love you.'

World Youth Day came to life on Palm Sunday 1984, during the Holy Year of Redemption, when thousands of young people marched through the city of Rome to St Peter's Square. It was an amazing event that moved many of the Roman onlookers to tears. Every Palm Sunday thereafter marked World Youth Day and the success of the gathering in Rome convinced the Pope to celebrate the event in different locations around the world: Buenos Aires (1987), Santiago de Compostela (1989), Czestochowa (1991), Denver (1993), Manila (1995), Paris (1997), Rome (2000) and Toronto (2002). World Youth Day is a legacy of John Paul II's papacy that continues under Pope Benedict XVI. John Paul wrote that:

> These World Youth Days have become a great and fascinating witness that young people give of themselves.

They have become a powerful means of evangelisation.
In the young there is ... an immense potential for good
and for creative possibility. Whenever I meet them in my
travels throughout the world, I wait first of all to hear what
they want to tell me about themselves, about their society,
about their Church. And I always point out: 'What I am
going to say to you is not as important as what you are
going to say to me. You will not necessarily say it to me
in words; you will say it to me by your presence, by your
song, perhaps by your dancing, by your skits, and finally
by your enthusiasm'. We need the enthusiasm of the
young.[155]

It was impressive to see John Paul join in the festivities with young
people – joking, clapping, singing. And yet he didn't pull punches. He
spoke clearly on issues to do with sexuality, the dignity of the person
and the nature of true freedom. Above all, it was the coherence between
what he said and how he lived that struck his young friends when he
spoke:

It is necessary to prepare young people for marriage, it is
necessary to teach them love. Love is not something that
is learned, and yet there is nothing else as important to
learn. As a young priest I learned to love human love.[156]

He also knew that young people had so much to give. He believed in their
ideals, generosity and exuberant joy. He knew how to point them towards
what remains beyond the disappointments of life, the counterfeits of truth
that are often sold to them and the consumerist mentality.

In 1985, during the International Youth Year, he wrote the letter
Dilecti Amici, in which he drew young people's attention to the
conversation between Jesus and the rich young man (cf. Mt 19:16-22).
He translated the young man's question, 'Good Teacher, what must I
do to inherit eternal life?' into the language of our times as, 'How must
I act so that my life will have meaning and value?'[157] Today, the future
holds many possibilities, choices and questions for young people, so it is
important that they hear Jesus' reply to the young man, 'No one is good
but God alone,' and understand it to mean that 'only God is the ultimate

basis of all values; only he gives the definitive meaning to our human existence.[158]

John Paul's hope was that young people would reflect on the plan for their lives and experience what the Gospel means when it says of Jesus' encounter with the young man: 'Jesus, looking upon him, loved him.' There's a passion in the Pope's words:

> May you experience a look like that! May you experience the truth that he, Christ, looks upon you with love! ... My wish for each of you is that you may discover this look of Christ, and experience it in all its depth. I do not know at what moment in your life. I think that it will happen when you need it most ... [159]

Pope John Paul encourages young people to make good choices, knowing that they are loved eternally and chosen from eternity. God has a unique, unrepeatable plan for each person – and it is always a plan of love.

A Great Witness to Sickness Lived in Faith
'Be able to find in love the salvific meaning of your pain'

On 13 May 1992, eleven years after the assassination attempt on his life that resulted in a period of prolonged suffering and a stay in hospital, Pope John Paul II announced that the Church would observe 11 February, the Feast day of Our Lady of Lourdes, as a special World Day of the Sick. Each year since, on that date, St Peter's Basilica is filled with people, many of whom are sick, and wheelchairs surround the high altar. Apart from being directed towards the sick, one of the aims of the day is to stimulate awareness of the serious and inescapable problems concerning health policy and care: about two-thirds of humankind still lack essential medical care, while the resources employed in this sector are often insufficient.

Although John Paul II was a man who became increasingly well acquainted with illness as his life went on, he once spoke about how sick people intimidated him when he was young and of how he had shied away from looking at those in pain. However, in later years he lived out his own suffering, illnesses and periods of hospitalisation in a very public manner. Indeed, just a few months after announcing the World Day of Sick, he himself fell very ill, reporting considerable stomach pain. X-rays showed that he had a tumour in the sigmoid flexure of the colon. His condition was serious and the seventy-two year old had to undergo an operation to remove an orange-sized pre-cancerous tumour. It was a potentially life-threatening four-hour operation. In order to reach the tumour, the surgeons had to re-open the scar left from the surgery that had been carried out after the assassination attempt in 1981. In the course of the operation they discovered gallstones and also removed the gallbladder. Subsequently, a biopsy indicated that the tumour was turning cancerous. The Pope recovered well from the operation and even undertook new commitments and trips, but then on 11 November 1993, he tripped in the Hall of Benediction in the Apostolic Palace after an audience with officials of the UN Food and Agriculture Organisation, dislocating his right shoulder and suffering a slight fracture to its socket. His arms and shoulder were immobilised and he wore a sling for about four weeks.

On 28 April 1994, he slipped again in the bathroom of his apartment, suffering a transcervical fracture under the head of the right femur, and underwent hip-replacement surgery. Throughout that year he was in serious pain, walking slowly and carrying a stick publicly for the first time. He became visibly and audibly weaker, and looking back later, it was clear that Parkinson's had set in.

Pope John Paul persevered, believing that though illness in itself is a limit and absurdity, because of Jesus Christ, suffering can be transformed by love. The current spokesperson for the Vatican, Father Lombardi, has characterised John Paul II as a 'great witness to sickness lived in faith'.[160] Taking up Paul's notion of 'completing the suffering of Christ for the benefit of his Body which is the Church' (cf. Col 1:24), the Pope believed that the pain and suffering that come with illness can be salvific:

> Dear people who are sick, be able to find in love 'the salvific meaning of your pain and valid answers to all your questions'. Yours is a mission of most lofty value for both the Church and society. 'You that bear the weight of suffering occupy the first places among those whom God loves. As with all those he met along the roads of Palestine, Jesus directs a gaze full of tenderness at you; his love will never be lacking.' Manage to be generous witnesses to this privileged love through the gift of your suffering, which can do so much for the salvation of the human race.[161]

Having uttered so many words of comfort and encouragement to the sick throughout his years as Pope, it was appropriate that John Paul's last international journey, which took place on 14–15 August 2004, was to Lourdes, the great Marian shrine to which so many sick make a pilgrimage. As everyone could see that day, he himself was now suffering greatly, an ill man among the ill offering his living testimony of faith, hope and love: find in love the salvific meaning of your pain.

The Theology of the Body
'Tell the truth with our bodies'

In the course of some 129 general audiences, beginning on 5 September 1979 and continuing until 28 November 1984, Pope John Paul II surprised many with his reflections on the 'theology of the body'. Yet it was a theme that he had begun to reflect upon as a young pastor in Poland. His message was clear: our body speaks! It has a language. It whispers God's plan to us. The body is Good News.

In the past, Christians risked presenting faith only in intellectual or spiritual-interior terms. It was said they actually had a 'fear of the flesh' and the body was, at times, a neglected theme in Christian reflection. Questions such as the meaning of human love, the reason why God created us male and female, and the purpose of the gift of sex were not explored in depth.

Reading the Genesis accounts in the light of Jesus Christ who gave his life for the Church (Eph 5:31-2), John Paul views the complementarity of the sexes as a sign that each of us has been created, not to live simply for oneself in solitude, but rather to be a gift for others. In this sense, John Paul speaks of the 'nuptial meaning' of the body. Sexual drive and the desire to be in relationship are deep signs of the profound capacity each of us has for expressing love: 'that love in which we become gift and through this gift realize the very meaning of our existence'.[162] It is the love of self-surrender, of going outside of and abandoning oneself in love to the other, of being willing to make oneself belong to the other. The nuptial meaning of our body is at the service of mutual self-surrender in mutual love.[163]

The sexual intimacy of man and woman is meant to express exclusive spousal love, because body, spirit and personhood are all interlinked. In the 'original innocence' and 'original nakedness', the first man and woman did not experience shame because they could see in each other's body another person and their masculinity and femininity was in the service of love. Their bodies expressed them, their sexual energy was taken up in spousal love. It was sin that introduced a split in the body–soul unity, resulting in desire for the other sexually, but without seeing the other as person. It is in redemption that we discover again the reintegration of bodily sexuality and personhood. In a retreat for students in March 1954, Karol Wojtyła explained:

> Sexual drive is a gift from God. Many may offer this drive to God exclusively through a vow of virginity. A person may offer it to another human being with the awareness that he/she is offering it to a person. It must not be a matter of chance. On the other side there is another human being who must not be hurt, whom one must love. Only a person can love a person. To love means to wish for the other person's good, to offer oneself for the good of the other. When a new life is to come into being as the result of the act of giving oneself, this must be a gift of the person given out of love. In this area one must not separate love from the [sexual] drive ... If we respect the sexual drive within love, we will not violate love, we will not bring love to ruination.[164]

According to John Paul, we always have a choice – to either tell the truth with our bodies (in the way we use them), or to lie. For him, telling the truth with our body is as important as telling the truth with our voice. For instance, to give your body to someone who is not your spouse is a form of lie because you are offering the new partner something that in justice belongs to someone else or that is not yet fully ready to be given.

It is clear that the Pope understood this to be a difficult and delicate topic – the range of questions that had surfaced in the context of Pope Paul VI's encyclical *Humanae Vitae* in 1968 was evidence of that. In the extended series of addresses on the 'theology of the body' given between 1979 and 1984, John Paul II offered a profound overview of the beauty of God's project for man and woman as sexually embodied beings, and explained how that impacts on the many questions surrounding pre-marital sex, contraception, adultery and homosexuality.

In his 'theology of the body', John Paul II invites us to reflect on primordial human experiences and consider them within a framework offered by revelation.

7

Building the Civilisation of Love

'As far as the Church is concerned, the social message of the Gospel must not be considered a theory, but above all else a basis and a motivation for action ... The newness which is experienced in following Christ demands to be communicated to ... people in their concrete difficulties, struggles, problems and challenges.'

~ *Centesimus Annus*

Serving Humanity: Culture, History, Liberation
'Only love constructs ... hatred destroys'

Among the many themes that John Paul II reflected upon, the topics of history and time, culture and nation, democracy and political systems loom large. As he put it, 'In Christianity time [and so history and culture] has a fundamental importance ... In Jesus Christ, the Word made flesh, time becomes a dimension of God.'[165] His starting point on this topic is often the opening account of creation in the Book of Genesis where we read of humanity being entrusted with stewardship of the world: 'Be fruitful and multiply, and fill the earth and subdue it; and have dominion over the fish of the sea' (Gen 1:28).

As the Pope explained, in these first words of the Bible we find:

> ... the earliest and most complete definition of human culture. To subdue and have dominion over the earth means to discover and confirm the truth about being human, about the humanity that belongs equally to man and to woman. To us and to our humanity, God has entrusted the visible world as a gift and also as a task. In other words, he has assigned us a particular mission: to accomplish the truth about ourselves and about our world.[166]

From the outset, then, as builders of civilisation, we are shaping culture through our life as members of families, peoples, nations and states.

In an address to UNESCO, speaking about his own beloved Poland, John Paul affirmed:

> I am the son of a nation which has lived the greatest experiences of history, which its neighbours have condemned to death several times, but which has survived and remained itself. It has kept its identity, and it has kept, in spite of partitions and foreign occupations, its national sovereignty, not by relying on the resources of physical

power, but solely by relying on its culture. This culture
turned out in the circumstances to be more powerful than
all other forces.[167]

In building up civilisation, humanity has been given a model. Whereas
in creating other beings, God simply says 'Let there be ...' In the case
of humanity it is as if he 'goes back into himself for a kind of Trinitarian
consultation and then decides: "Let us make humankind in our image,
according to our likeness" (Gen 1:26)'.[168] For the Pope, it is precisely the
fact of being created and continuously created in the image and likeness
of God who is Love – the Trinity of divine persons who love one
another – that we find the truth about ourselves, our culture, our nation
and our society. It is the horizon against which we make our decisions
and act.

The life of love found in the Trinity is the eternal law that supports
the natural law to which we are all attuned and in accordance with
which we are called to shape civilisation. The Trinity proposes a model
of relationships between peoples and nations that is respectful of the
distinctive features of each people or community as well as being
committed to globalisation. This is the basis of the twin principles of
solidarity and subsidiarity.

In a talk he gave early in his pontificate, John Paul proclaimed the
social power that can be unleashed from love:

> ... love constructs; only love constructs! Hatred destroys.
> Hatred does not construct anything. It can only
> disintegrate. It can disorganise social life ... For Rome, for
> my new Diocese, and at the same time for the whole of the
> Church and for the world, I desire love and justice. Justice
> and love, so that we may be able to construct.[169]

By bringing the truth of the Gospel of love and justice, Christians can
offer a light that liberates and helps culture reach its fulfilment:

> The Gospel is not opposed to any culture, as if in engaging
> a culture the Gospel would seek to strip it of its native
> riches and force it to adopt forms which are alien to it.
> On the contrary, the message which believers bring to the

world and to cultures is a genuine liberation from all the
disorders caused by sin and is, at the same time, a call to
the fullness of truth. Cultures are not only not diminished
by this encounter; rather, they are prompted to open
themselves to the newness of the Gospel's truth and to be
stirred by this truth to develop in new ways.[170]

John Paul was well aware of the crisis of contemporary Western
culture, not least as it enters into dialogue with other cultures in a new
worldwide cultural context. He attempted to remind the West that it
shares in the basic common quest of humanity and that it is by getting
in touch with this shared quest that it will find its bearings again at the
beginning of the third millennium. In the opening lines of *Fides et Ratio,*
he writes:

In both East and West, we may trace a journey which has
led humanity down the centuries to meet and engage truth
more and more deeply ... Moreover, a cursory glance at
ancient history shows clearly how in different parts of the
world, with their different cultures, there arise at the same
time the fundamental questions which pervade human life:
*Who am I? Where have I come from and where am I going?
Why is there evil? What is there after this life?* These are the
questions which we find in the sacred writings of Israel,
as also in the Veda and the Avesta; we find them in the
writings of Confucius and Lao-Tze, and in the preaching
of Tirthankara and Buddha; they appear in the poetry of
Homer and in the tragedies of Euripides and Sophocles, as
they do in the philosophical writings of Plato and Aristotle.
They are questions which have their common source in the
quest for meaning which has always compelled the human
heart. In fact, the answer given to these questions decides
the direction which people seek to give to their lives.[171]

The Church has its role to play within this search, as he puts it:

The Church is no stranger to this journey of discovery ...
the Church has made her pilgrim way along the paths of

the world to proclaim that Jesus Christ is 'the way, and
the truth, and the life' (Jn 14:6). It is her duty to serve
humanity in different ways, but one way in particular
imposes a responsibility of a quite special kind: the
diakonia [service] *of the truth*.[172]

In the service of the truth, Christianity has played an important role in
uniting different cultures in a common civilisation. In the contemporary
intersection of cultures, economic, political or entertainment inter-
nationalisms are not enough. Christianity is called today to offer a
genuine 'DNA' for a universal humanity, a Trinitarian vision and life,
one that can animate a civilisation of love.[173]

War and Peace
'No to War! War is not always inevitable. It is always a defeat for humanity'

In his messages for the annual World Day of Peace, we hear a constant echo of Pope John Paul II's conviction that war, in all its forms, is a defeat for humanity. He stresses that in war it is the civilian population, especially children and women, who suffer the most. War results in poverty and poverty breeds war. Furthermore war gives rise to macabre scenarios, the memory of which can damage people's ability to relate, thereby giving rise to further crises.

The Polish Pope who had experienced war first hand was, however, no naive pacifist. In his message for the Year 2000, he recognises that it is legitimate and even obligatory to take active measures to disarm the attacks of an unjust aggressor where political efforts and non-violent defence have proven to be of no avail. That said, John Paul was attentive to the rise in public opinion against war. He saw it as a sign of something new emerging in human history, a new consciousness of the need to resolve humanity's problems together. He often repeated his opinion that the media and communications networks in general play a very important role in this.

On 24 January 2002, once again gathering leaders of the world's religions together in Assisi to pray for peace, this time after the 9/11 attack, John Paul declared: 'Never again violence! Never again war! Never again terrorism!' In an address to the Diplomatic Corps on 13 January 2003, some months before the second war in Iraq, he spoke of war as a 'defeat for humanity' and pleaded for renewed international arrangements that can ensure peaceful co-existence between individuals, nations and peoples:

> 'NO TO WAR'! War is not always inevitable. It is
> always a defeat for humanity. International law, honest
> dialogue, solidarity between States, the noble exercise
> of diplomacy: these are methods worthy of individuals
> and nations in resolving their differences ... War is never

just another means that one can choose to employ for settling differences between nations. As the Charter of the United Nations Organisation and international law itself remind us, war cannot be decided upon, even when it is a matter of ensuring the common good, except as the very last option and in accordance with very strict conditions, without ignoring the consequences for the civilian population both during and after the military operations.[174]

John Paul didn't just say 'no to war'. He worked actively for peace. There were two sides to his commitment – teaching and practical initiatives. He repeatedly underlined the need for justice and freedom, truth and love. As Cardinal Sodano put it:

> The fall of the Berlin Wall was nothing short of a collapse of a spiritual way that was much greater than the material wall. The material wall had divided the German capital in two with a barrier of 154 kilometres, but the spiritual wall was much longer and it was eventually knocked down thanks to the constant work of John Paul II who never ceased to cry out against the absurdity of that system and plead for the right of people to freedom and, so, to social peace.[175]

As noted, John Paul made many pleas for peace during his many international journeys. Apart from his constant concern for such areas as the Holy Land, he also championed the cause of peace in the Balkans, Central Africa and Iraq. In Drogheda, Ireland, he is remembered for his passionate plea to those involved in conflict: 'On my knees I beg you to turn away from violence.'[176] In the context of the terrible fratricidal wars between Tutsi and Hutu in the region of the Great Lakes (Rwanda, Burundi and the Democratic Republic of Congo), that resulted in millions dead and two million refugees within a few short months in 1994, Pope John Paul II spoke out while the international world powers remained passive. And his contribution to conflict transformation in Latin America should not be forgotten: it was his mediation during the war between Argentina and Chile that resulted in a Peace Treaty in 1984 that still stands.

Towards the end of his life, and despite his failing energy, the Pope did all he could to prevent war in Iraq. He attempted direct mediation by sending Cardinal Roger Etchegaray as his personal representative to Baghdad, and Cardinal Pio Laghi to Washington to bring messages of peace to the countries' respective presidents, Saddam Hussein and George W. Bush. When war broke out on 20 March 2003, John Paul kept the nunciature open in Iraq, even during the bombing. It has been noted by observers of international politics that the Pope's repeated and passionate interventions meant that the war was not seen by Arab peoples or adherents of Islam as a war of Christians against Muslims, nor as a Western religious war against the Muslim world.

One particular feature of Pope John Paul II's commitment to peace was his promotion of the Catholic Church's social teaching. It is significant that in 2004, towards the end of his papacy, that the *Compendium of the Social Doctrine of the Church* was published. He brought new vigour and insight to the promotion of that teaching through his social encyclicals *Laborem Exercens* (1981), *Sollicitudo Rei Socialis* (1987), *Centesimus Annus* (1991).

In his 1986 message for the World day of Peace he concluded:

> To each one of you, young and old, weak and powerful, I appeal: embrace peace as the great unifying value of your lives ...
>
> Peace as a value with no frontiers:
> North-South, East-West,
> everywhere one people united in only one Peace.[177]

Dealing with Faults of the Past
'I ask forgiveness'

It has been said that forgiveness was an underlying theme of John Paul II's papacy.[178] Yet it is one that played a crucial role and that stemmed from his early life experiences. A visual image of John Paul's harsh personal experience of World War II is captured in the film *Karol: The Man Who Became Pope*.[179] In his own book, *Memory and Identity*, Pope John Paul recorded his experience of this period:

> It remains indelibly fixed in my memory ... We were totally swallowed up in a great eruption of evil and only gradually did we begin to realize its true nature ... Both the Nazis during the war and later, the Communists in Eastern Europe, tried to hide what they were doing from public opinion ... Yet it is hard to forget the evil that has been personally experienced: one can only forgive. And what does it mean to forgive, if not to appeal to a good that is greater than evil. This good, after all, has its foundation in God alone.[180]

After the assassination attempt on his life, he provided eloquent testimony to this conviction by extending forgiveness to his would-be assassin, Mehmet Ali Ağca. Years later, during a visit to Sarajevo, a city torn apart by a bitter civil war sparked by religious hatred, an enfeebled Pope John Paul II again called for forgiveness and reconciliation.

For John Paul forgiveness was not just a personal attitude but rather a social and political necessity. It is not a question of ignoring wrongdoing – justice requires acknowledgement of transgression. However, forgiveness also needs to be brought into play as a completion of justice. In this 2002 message for the World Day of Peace he stated:

> True peace therefore is the fruit of justice, that moral virtue and legal guarantee which ensures full respect for rights and responsibilities, and the just distribution of benefits and burdens. But because human justice is always

fragile and imperfect, subject as it is to the limitations
and egoism of individuals and groups, it must include
and, as it were, be completed by *the forgiveness which
heals and rebuilds troubled human relations from their
foundations.* This is true in circumstances great and small,
at the personal level or on a wider, even international
scale. Forgiveness is in no way opposed to justice, as if
to forgive meant to overlook the need to right the wrong
done. It is rather the fullness of justice, leading to that
tranquillity of order which is much more than a fragile
and temporary cessation of hostilities, involving as it does
the deepest healing of the wounds which fester in human
hearts. Justice and forgiveness are both essential to such
healing.[181]

In his second encyclical, *Dives in Misericordia,* John Paul had already
written on the need to introduce forgiveness into mutual relationships
in order to make society 'ever more human'. A world from which
forgiveness is eliminated would be 'nothing but a world of cold and
unfeeling justice, in the name of which each person would claim his or
her own rights vis-à- vis others'.[182] Human society would be turned into
a system of oppression of the weak by the strong, or into an arena of
permanent strife between one group and another.

Pope John Paul also highlighted the theme of forgiveness as a
necessity in reviewing the Church's own history. The journalist Luigi
Accattoli collected together the many pronouncements in which John
Paul sought forgiveness for Church misbehaviour through the centuries
in his 1998 book, *When a Pope Asks Forgiveness.* These pronouncements
cover a range of areas, including the Crusades, women, religious wars,
Galileo, Luther, the Jews, and the Inquisition.

In preparation for the Jubilee 2000 celebration, Pope John Paul
called for a study of the Church and the faults of the past. Some were
nervous of this proposal but the Pope persevered and a symposium
was held with top scholars and historians present. The International
Theological Commission also studied the subject and published a
document, *Memory and Reconciliation: The Church and the Faults of the
Past.*[183] This document responds to questions that had arisen about the
Pope's many requests for forgiveness for faults of the past. It clarifies
the reasons, the conditions, and the exact form of these requests and

provides many interesting points on how to read history and interpret theologically the issue of forgiveness for past faults.

In March 2000, the Pope celebrated a ceremony seeking forgiveness of the Church's misdeeds throughout the centuries. It was a high point in the healing of memory process that he had begun several years previously:

> Brothers and Sisters, let us turn with trust to God our
> Father, who is merciful and compassionate, slow to
> anger, great in love and fidelity, and ask him to accept the
> repentance of his people who humbly confess their sins,
> and to grant them mercy.[184]

It was John Paul II's hope that the healing of historical memory and forgiveness would spread as a culture, and also in the political arena, within and between nations.

The World of Work
'Co-creators with God through work'

Some of the photographs from Karol Wojtyła's early adulthood are from his years working in the stone quarry and water purification facility at the Solvay plant. Only later did he realise how important this experience was for him:

> Having worked with my hands, I knew quite well the meaning of physical labour. Every day I had been with people who did heavy work. I came to know their living situations, their families, their interests, their human worth, and their dignity ... I made friends with the workers. Sometimes they invited me to their homes ... These contacts ... remained very close.[185]

During his studies in Rome he got to know about worker-priests and the Young Christian Worker movement and began to reflect on how important the world of work had become for the Church and the priests in the West.

In his encyclical *Laborem Exercens*, Pope John Paul wrote that, in the light of the creation account, we can see that it is through work that we become the image of God:

> Men and women are the image of God partly through the mandate received from their Creator to subdue, to dominate, the earth. In carrying out this mandate, humankind, every human being, reflects the very action of the Creator of the universe.[186]

Work is not a senseless exercise. It is the means for becoming God's image. Unlike the people of the ancient world, where manual labour was believed to be dishonourable or demeaning, Christians have a strong work ethic. Workers are the image of God and his co-workers in creation. Workers are persons with dignity regardless of what the objective content of their work is. They collaborate in the world's development. As John Paul explains, work is for humankind, humankind is not for work:

> Work is a good thing for man – a good thing for his humanity – because through work man *not only transforms nature,* adapting it to his own needs, but he also *achieves fulfilment* as a human being and indeed, in a sense, becomes 'more a human being'. (6)

Clearly, if the human person becomes more fully human in the image of God through work, then the lack of a job is a serious matter both in terms of a person's potential for development and their participation in the community. Those in positions of responsibility in society and government need to see to it that those who want work can find a job.

Christians are called to humanise working conditions, because to permit conditions that are unworthy of human beings is to be guilty of a sin against humanity created in the image of God. As is stated in *Laborem Exercens,* 'we must first of all recall a principle that has always been taught by the Church: *the principle of the priority of labour over capital*' (12). Business and economics should be structured to make sure that the law of economic returns (itself important) should not be at the expense of the human dignity of the individual.

In order to exercise their freedom, employees should be allowed a reasonable role of co-determination and responsibility in the workplace:

> ... the person who works desires *not only* due *remuneration* for his work; he also wishes that, within the production process, provision be made for him to be able to *know* that in his work, even on something that is owned in common, he is working '*for himself*. (15)

In short, in terms of building the civilisation of love, work is one of the perennial and fundamental aspects that are always relevant and constantly demanding renewed attention and decisive witness.

Poverty, Economics and Solidarity
'There's an urgent need to re-think the economy'

Alongside the imposing building in Rome that houses the Congregation for the Doctrine of Faith, stands a modest building that Pope John Paul gave to the Mother Teresa Sisters. It was a gesture that spoke volumes: faith works through charity! But charity, for John Paul II, was not merely philanthropy or a little bit of almsgiving. Taking his lead from the account of the Last Judgement in Matthew's Gospel, he indicates that it has to do with the very mystery of Jesus Christ present in every human being – especially the poor, marginalised and ignored:

> I was hungry and you gave me food, I was thirsty and you gave me drink, I was a stranger and you welcomed me, I was naked and you clothed me, I was sick and you visited me, I was in prison and you came to me (Mt 25:35-7).

Whatever we do to our neighbour, Jesus views as done to him. Fidelity to Jesus Christ, therefore, is clearly measured in the Church, the Bride of Christ, not just in terms of the orthodoxy of doctrine but also in terms of our relationship to Christ in the poor.

From his earliest years, Pope John Paul was confronted with the issue of poverty.[187] In 1939, during the war, he wrote to one of his great theatre friends, Kotlarczyk: 'life in Cracow if you can imagine, consists of queues for bread and of rather rare expeditions for sugar ... and of black nostalgia for coal ... and of reading.'[188] The idealistic nineteen year old wrote of Poland, the land he loved so dearly, as suffering terrible injustice 'because the peasant was killed and imprisoned for demanding his just rights from the government ... He was right and he had the law on his side, [but] the nation was misled and lied to.' He knew that totalitarian regimes were counterfeits and wrote to Kotlarczyk: 'our liberation must be the gateway of Christ'. It was 'the greatness of Christianity' that would keep the ideal of justice alive. When liberation theology became popular many years later, especially in South America, the problem for John Paul was certainly not liberation or concern for or identification with the poor, but rather the fact that a failed ideology – Marxism with its class struggle and engendering of hatred – was being used as the framework for theology.

Sometimes John Paul was considered idealistic in his social doctrine. For instance, in *Sollicitudo Rei Socialis* (1987) he affirmed strongly that there was a need to transform the two socio-economic and ideological systems dominant at the time – liberal capitalism and Marxist collectivism. At that point it seemed the two blocs were fixed features of world order and it was hard to see how they could overcome, although John Paul proposed that this was a necessary condition for the realisation of significant development. At best, this was seen as a perfect ideal.

While he recognised the impossibility of reaching perfection until the new heaven and new earth, Pope John Paul proposed the need to keep striving to build up ever more perfect expressions of a true and just society: what we build in love in this world we will find in the next.

Sollicitudo Rei Socialis takes up the themes of poverty and development that had been expounded in the encyclical *Populorum Progressio*, and analyses poverty as a structural phenomenon of industrial society. John Paul goes so far as to speak of 'structural sins' that must be overcome not by almsgiving or occasional acts of solidarity, but rather by an equally structured solidarity, capable of building up structures that are human – what might be called 'structures of grace'.[189]

In his message for the annual World Day of Peace published on 12 December 1992, John Paul presented poverty as a cause of conflicts that in turn increase poverty, thereby generating a vicious circle. But he also challenged us to escape from this circle by the free choice of a positive poverty – a moderate and simplistic lifestyle – to give greater wealth to the elimination of unjust poverty. The encyclical *Centesimus Annus* continues this line of thought in terms of ecology, stating that 'this may mean making important changes in established lifestyles, in order to limit the waste of environmental and human resources, thus enabling every individual and all peoples of the earth to have a sufficient share of those resources'.[190]

John Paul recognised the urgent need to rethink the economy, considering both the dramatic material poverty of billions of people in the world and the fact that 'present economic, social and cultural structures are ill-equipped to meet the demands of genuine development'.[191] He affirmed that current models of economic and social development need to be reassessed in light of the dignity of individuals and peoples and spoke of the need for a 'preferential option for the poor' in addressing social, political and economic issues.

Of course, John Paul recognised that economies need to work and be efficient. Free initiative, creativity and enterprise are to be encouraged. But he was convinced that the requirements of social justice need to be better harmonised with other economic goals. As the *Compendium of the Social Doctrine of the Church* states: 'Economists ... and political leaders must sense the urgency of rethinking the economy'. Here he underlined in particular 'solidarity', which must, he proposed, be part of networks of economic, political and social interdependence that the current process of globalisation tends to consolidate.[192] As in the case of many other topics, Pope John Paul II looked in hope to Christian associations that are active in the economic field and made up of workers, business leaders and economists, for new initiatives and ideas.

Grave Issues Facing Humanity
'The Gospel of life is at the heart of Jesus' message'

Life is a central theme running like a gold thread through all of John Paul's teaching. He was known for his strong defence of the value and inviolability of human life at every stage. In his 1995 encyclical letter, *Evangelium Vitae*, which he was asked to write by the world's bishops, he begins with the words: 'The Gospel of life is at the heart of Jesus' message. Lovingly received day after day by the Church, it is to be preached with dauntless fidelity as "good news" to the people of every age and culture.'[193] The religion editor of *Newsweek*, Kenneth Woodward, praised the letter calling it 'the clearest, most impassioned and most commanding encyclical' that Pope John Paul had written, one that would be his 'signature statement' in history.[194] In it, John Paul courageously identified and explored the gravest questions facing humanity.

On the one hand, the encyclical is a clear response to old and new threats to human life. It not only highlights 'the fact of the destruction of so many human lives still to be born or in their final stage', but also the equally 'grave and disturbing ... fact that conscience itself ... is finding it increasingly difficult to distinguish between good and evil in what concerns the basic value of human life'.[195]

John Paul provides a profound meditation on what life is, as presented to us in Scripture. He brings us to see that we are called in God's plan not simply to obey the commandment not to kill human life, but also to revere life, to love it, protect it and foster it.

There are many areas that he addresses. One key issue, for instance, is how our contemporary understanding of democracy often betrays its foundation when it recognises in law the killing of the defenceless and the weakest in society: 'To claim the right to abortion, infanticide and euthanasia, and to recognise that right in law, means to attribute to human freedom a perverse and evil significance: that of an absolute power over others and against others. This is the death of true freedom.'[196] The root cause of all of this, in John Paul's view, is the eclipse of God from the horizon of people's thought and decision. As

the Second Vatican Council put it: 'Without the Creator the creature
would disappear ... But when God is forgotten the creature itself grows
unintelligible.'[197] Responding to what he calls 'the culture of death', John
Paul believes we need to repropose God, bringing people to rediscover
God, who is Love and source of all life, and so propose a 'culture of
life' that has the dignity of every human being created by God at its
foundation.

With regard to the death penalty, he writes:

> There is evidence of a growing public opposition to the
> death penalty, even when such a penalty is seen as a kind
> of 'legitimate defence' on the part of society. Modern
> society in fact has the means of effectively suppressing
> crime by rendering criminals harmless without
> definitively denying them the chance to reform.[198]

Pope John Paul is well known for his strong stance in defence of the
unborn. In his 1994 Christmas Eve address to the Vatican Curia, he
referred to his encyclical on life, pointing out that the Church had made
its voice heard in order to awaken people's conscience. He quoted Mother
Teresa of Calcutta: 'not the mother, not the father, not the doctor, not
an agency, not a conference, not a government, has the right to end a life
– only God who has created it'. John Paul is aware, of course, that often
women have to face difficult decisions, having been abandoned by men
unwilling to accept responsibility for a child they have fathered, and that
women can be under direct or indirect pressure to get rid of a child.[199]

Writing on the difficult issue of what to do when legislative or political
choices contrary to Christian principle and values of life are proposed,
taking the example of abortion, John Paul provides the following
guideline: when it is not possible to avoid the implementation of such
laws, a parliamentary representative, whose personal opposition to the
law is clear, may legitimately support proposals aimed at limiting the harm
caused by the law or programme. The vote would not be in support of an
unjust law such as that of abortion, but rather a contribution to reducing
the negative consequences of the legislative provision: 'This does not
in fact represent an illicit cooperation with an unjust law, but rather a
legitimate and proper attempt to limit its evil aspects.'[200]

On the issue of medical treatment for someone who is terminally ill, where the medical procedures have become disproportionate to any expected results or impose an excessive burden on the patient and his family, Pope John Paul repeats the Catholic position that medical treatment may be discontinued. When death is clearly imminent and inevitable, 'one can in conscience refuse forms of treatment that would only secure a precarious and burdensome prolongation of life, so long as the normal care due to the sick person in similar cases is not interrupted' (65).

While *Evangelium Vitae* addressed very grave issues, John Paul II was always a man of hope. He notes positively the many movements or initiatives that work to promote life. He praises 'those daily gestures of openness, sacrifice and unselfish care which countless people lovingly make in families, hospitals, orphanages, homes for the elderly and other centres or communities which defend life' (27). It is known, for instance, that Catholic organisations provide around twenty-five percent of the care received by Aids victims worldwide. The Pope also saw as positive the fact that there is a 'sensitivity ever more opposed to war as an instrument for the resolution of conflicts between peoples' and the growing attention being paid to quality of life and to ecology. He also welcomed a reawakening of ethical reflection on life issues:

> The emergence and ever more widespread development
> of bioethics is promoting more reflection and dialogue
> between believers and non-believers, as well as between
> followers of different religions on ethical problems,
> including fundamental issues pertaining to human life. (27)

Women in Society and in the Church
'The journey must go on ...'

Throughout his many years as Pope, John Paul was very much aware of the need to reflect on and act much more incisively in promoting the role of women at every level in society and in the Church. Two documents in particular stand out – the 1988 apostolic letter on the dignity of women, *Mulieris Dignitatem*, and the 1995 *Letter to Women*.[201]

Reacting in surprise to *Mulieris Dignitatem*, French newspaper *Le Monde* described it as a re-reading of the Bible from a woman's perspective. It noted the Pope's explanation of St Paul, who is often depicted as saying that women are to be submissive to men. John Paul explained the Pauline text in terms of submission of man and woman to each other in the relationship of mutual love. The relationship between man and woman is characterised by complementarity and reciprocity. Chapter five of *Mulieris Dignitatem* has been praised for its account of the Gospel presentation of Jesus' relationship with women. John Paul affirms that Jesus' way of acting – the Gospel of his words and deeds – 'is a consistent *protest* against whatever offends the dignity of women'.[202] He highlights how Jesus deplores violence against women in the area of sexuality.

In his *Letter to Women*, the Pope acknowledges how in history the progress of women has frequently been blocked:

> Women's dignity has often been unacknowledged and their prerogatives misrepresented; they have often been relegated to the margins of society and even reduced to servitude. This has prevented women from truly being themselves and it has resulted in a spiritual impoverishment of humanity.[203]

He also remarked:

> I cannot fail to express my admiration for those women of good will who have devoted their lives to defending

the dignity of womanhood by fighting for their basic
social, economic and political rights, demonstrating
courageous initiative at a time when this was considered
extremely inappropriate, the sign of a lack of femininity, a
manifestation of exhibitionism, and even a sin! (6)

There is an urgent need, he writes, to achieve real equality in every area:
equal pay for equal work, protection for working mothers, fairness in
career advancements, equality of spouses with regard to family rights
and the recognition of everything that is part of the rights and duties of
citizens in a democratic state. So he calls for 'an effective and intelligent
campaign for the promotion of women, concentrating on all areas of
women's life and beginning with a *universal recognition of the dignity of
women*' (6). John Paul was convinced that 'Women will increasingly
play a part in the solution of the serious problems of the future' (4).

In his Angelus Message of 16 July 1995, he affirmed that 'without
the contribution of women, society is less alive, culture is poorer, peace
more insecure.'[204] On 14 August 1995, he commented that women
often have to carry 'unbearable burdens' arising from indifference or
inadequate help. These burdens are compounded by legislation that
is insensitive to the value of the family and by a widespread culture
that renders men less responsible and, in the worst scenario, leads
them to view woman simply as objects of pleasure or as reproductive
instruments.[205]

In the lead up to the Fourth World Conference on Women to be
held in Beijing in 1995, the Pope reflected on the topic each Sunday
during August that year. He spoke of the need to let the 'genius of
women' be more fully expressed in the arenas of economics and politics,
and the life of society as a whole.

John Paul also recognised that female genius needs to be expressed
and valued more in the life of the Church. From the evidence of the
Gospel, it is clear that the Church at its origin differed from the culture
of the time and called women to tasks connected with spreading the
Gospel. In his letters, the Apostle Paul cites a great number of women
who had various functions in service of the early Christian community
(cf. Rom 16:1-15; Phil 4:2-3; Col 4:15 and 1 Cor 11:5; 1 Tim 5:16).

While he declared in the 1994 document *Ordinatio Sacerdotalis* that the 'Church has no authority ... to confer priestly ordination on women', John Paul was very clear that much more needed to be done regarding the role of women in the life of the Church.[206] In his letter on consecrated life, *Vita Consecrata*, he wrote that 'it is ... urgently necessary to take certain concrete steps, beginning by *providing room for women to participate* in different fields and at all levels, including decision-making processes, above all in matters which concern women themselves'.[207]

In terms of 'rewriting' history (there's a need to 'invert the tendency' of men writing history, as he put it on one occasion), John Paul highlighted the role of Brigid of Sweden, Catherine of Siena and Edith Stein as patrons of Europe and declared Teresa of Lisieux a Doctor of the Church. He often referred to women saints and mystics in his homilies and addresses and beatified or canonised many women. He appointed women to positions in the Vatican Curia and as auditors at the synods. And he chose Mary Anne Glendon to lead the Vatican delegation at the Beijing United Nations Conference on women.

Nevertheless, he himself was aware these were only first steps. 'This journey must go on!' he comments in his *Letter to Women* (6). Ultimately, however, what comes across in his teaching is that attempts to promote the true identity of women must not be reduced to strategic moves. It will emerge from women themselves, and they will reveal more of their genius as they engage in the service of love, crossing paths with Jesus Christ in today's world.

Referring to Mary, John Paul pointed out that love is the essential value for everyone: 'to serve is to reign' (10). He viewed women as the guardians of primary values and, above all, of the value of love which must be foremost in the Church. Everything else will pass away. Only love remains. Pope John Paul considered women as linked particularly to the Church's Marian profile which he defined as perhaps its 'most fundamental dimension' – a profile that is emerging gradually.

The *Letter to Artists*
'I feel closely linked to artists'

As has been noted, from his earliest years Karol Wojtyła nurtured a love of the arts, particularly drama. In his *Letter to Artists* on 4 April 1999, Pope John Paul reveals how he 'feels closely linked to artists ... by experiences reaching far back in time which have indelibly marked my life'.[208]

The Pope wrote his first play, *David* (which was subsequently lost), at the age of nineteen. Soon after, he translated Sophocles' *Oedipus Rex* from Greek into Polish. He founded the Rhapsodic Theatre along with others in 1941, during the German occupation of Poland, where works of the Polish Romantics were performed employing a dramatic theory imbued with principles of art and aesthetics, drama and poetry, philosophy, theology, and even linguistics. Wojtyła described this theatre as starting with 'the living word, spoken by people in extrascenic conditions, in a room with a piano. The unheard-of scarcity of the means of expression [because of the war] turned into a creative experiment'.[209] As a bishop, he would continue to write plays. Among his best known dramatic works are *Our God's Brother* (c. 1949), *The Jeweller's Shop* (1960), and *Radiation of Fatherhood* (1964). His poem, 'Roman Triptych', was published in 2003.

He dedicated his *Letter to Artists* to all who search for what he calls 'new "epiphanies" of beauty', because artists are by nature 'alert to every "epiphany" of the inner beauty of things' (6). They possess artistic creativity as a gift and it is this that appealed to John Paul II. Indeed, he viewed the artist as the image of God the Creator:

> None can sense more deeply than you artists ...
> something of the pathos with which God at the dawn of
> creation looked upon the work of his hands. A glimmer
> of that feeling has shone so often in your eyes when ...
> captivated by the hidden power of sounds and words,
> colours and shapes, you have admired the work of your
> inspiration, sensing in it some echo of the mystery of

creation with which God, the sole creator of all things, has
wished in some way to associate you. (1)

Every artist expresses themselves through their work, and all of us are
in some way artists in that we are all entrusted with the task of crafting
our own life, of making it 'a work of art, a masterpiece'. Nevertheless
John Paul is clear that 'not all are called to be artists in the special sense
of the term' (2). The gift of an artistic talent calls for responsibility.
If anyone has been endowed with the gift of being a poet or writer,
sculptor or architect, musician or actor, it is important 'not to waste that
talent but to develop it, in order to put it at the service of neighbour
and of humanity as a whole' (3). After all, 'Society needs artists, just as
it needs scientists, technicians, workers, professional people, witnesses
of the faith, teachers, fathers and mothers' who contribute to 'the art of
education' (4).

John Paul reviews the history of art in its various phases – ancient,
medieval and modern. He believed the history of art speaks to us today,
that through it we hear our brothers and sisters from the past utter a
message:

> ... through his works, the artist speaks to others and
> communicates with them. The history of art, therefore,
> is not only a story of works produced but also a story of
> men and women. Works of art speak of their authors;
> they enable us to know their inner life, and they reveal the
> original contribution which artists offer to the history of
> culture. (2)

True art can never simply be art for its own sake. It is always at the
service of beauty, truth and goodness. John Paul quotes Plato – 'The
power of the Good has taken refuge in the nature of the Beautiful' – and
the Polish poet Cyprian Norwid, who wrote that 'beauty is to enthuse
us to work, and work is to raise us up' (3).

It comes as no surprise then to note that Pope John Paul II thought
of art as 'a kind of bridge to religious experience':

> In so far as it seeks the beautiful, fruit of an imagination
> which arises above the everyday, art is by its nature a kind

of appeal to the mystery. Even when they explore the darkest depths of the soul or the most unsettling aspects of evil, artists give voice in a way to the universal desire for redemption. (10)

Therefore, art plays an important role in the civilisation of love: 'Humanity in every age, and even today, looks to works of art to shed light upon its path and its destiny' (14).

8

Towards Eternal Life

'Let us go forth full of trust in Christ. He will accompany us as we
journey toward the goal that he alone knows.'

~ *Rise, Let Us Be On Our Way*

The *Letter to the Elderly*
'The Pope is old and a little tired'

At a certain point during the Toronto World Youth Day in 2002, John Paul II movingly confided in his young listeners: 'You are young, the Pope is old and a little tired.' For all who had known him as energetic, sport-loving and fit in the earlier part of his pontificate, seeing him grow old struck chords of empathy as well as admiration for this man who still managed to identify with young people. Even some of those who had been his critics admitted that 'it did something to them' to see him gradually lose strength and become feeble. The Psalms say it so eloquently: 'Seventy is the sum of our years, or eighty if we are strong, and most of them are fruitless toil, for they pass quickly and we drift away' (Ps 90:10).

As he grew old, Pope John Paul continued believing in the love of God and saw opportunities even in his advanced years. And so, in 1999, he wrote a letter addressed to the elderly, a letter that reads like a one-to-one conversation: 'As an older person myself, I have felt the desire to engage in a conversation with you.'[210] There's something poignant about the way he says:

> I wish simply to express my spiritual closeness to you as someone who, with the passing of the years, has come to a deeper personal understanding of this phase of life and consequently feels a need for closer contact with other people of his own age, so that we can reflect together on the things we have in common. (1)

Quoting the Latin writer, Cicero, he acknowledges that old age is the 'autumn of life', but that this need not be a gloomy thought. Rather, John Paul is firm in his conviction that all contempt for the later years of life is misplaced:

> ... whereas childhood and youth are the times when the human person is being formed and is completely directed towards the future, and – in coming to appreciate his or

her own abilities – makes plans for adulthood, old age is
not without its own benefits. As St Jerome observes, with
the quieting of the passions, it 'increases wisdom, and
brings more mature counsels'. (5)

He recognises that in old age 'it is natural to revisit the past in order to
attempt a sort of assessment'. Looking back, many people and situations
come to mind. Dark moments of pain can disturb. But yet it is also true
that 'The passage of time helps us to see our experiences in a clearer
light and softens their painful side' (2). Experience is the great teacher,
it helps us see how daily difficulties, by God's grace, have contributed to
our growth and to the forging of our character.

As we grow old, the great hope of the resurrection becomes even
more important: 'we are consoled by the thought that, by virtue of our
spiritual souls, we will survive beyond death itself'. Quoting Irenaeus,
one of the earliest Christian writers, the Pope gives the reason for hope:
Jesus Christ 'became a man among men, in order to join the beginning
to the end, man to God' (2). There is a natural rebellion against
death, but God is the God of the living. And Jesus, having crossed the
threshold of death, has shown us the life of the resurrection beyond.

The Bible itself provides us with examples of 'elderly people' who
played an important part in God's plan: Abraham, Moses, Elizabeth and
Zechariah, Simeon and Anna, Nicodemus, and the elderly Peter. And so
the Pope writes: 'How reassuring are all these examples! They remind us
that at every stage of life the Lord can ask each of us to contribute what
talents we have. The service of the Gospel has nothing to do with age!'
(7).

Naturally, the Pope is particularly moved by the episode where Peter,
in his old age, is called to bear witness to his faith by martyrdom. Jesus
had once said to him: 'When you were young you girded yourself and
walked where you would; but when you are old, you will stretch out
your hands, and another will gird you and carry you where you do not
wish to go' (Jn 21:18). Pope John Paul says, 'These are words which ...
touch me personally; they make me feel strongly the need to reach out
and grasp the hands of Christ, in obedience to his command: "Follow
me!" (Jn 21:19)' (7).

The words of Psalm ninety-two also offer consolation: 'The just will
flourish like the palm-tree ... still bearing fruit when they are old, still full

of sap, still green, to proclaim that the Lord is just' (vv. 13, 15-16). The elderly have an important place in society. They are the guardians of our collective memory, and thus the privileged interpreters of that body of ideals and common values which support and guide life in society.

Growing old must have been painful for Pope John Paul II. He had been so active throughout his papacy – making international visits, writing documents, holding audiences and reorganising the Roman Curia – but now decisions had to be put off or left to collaborators. Yet he understood that what matters in growing old is to abandon ourselves into the loving and merciful hands of God the Father, not only by praying, but by serving in love as much as we can those who surround us at this time of life.[211]

Of course, it is also true that as we get older death is gradually approaching. In his *Letter to the Elderly*, the Pope shares a prayer that he found himself reciting more frequently in his advancing years: 'at the hour of my death, call me and bid me come to you' (17-18). He also reminds us of Mary's closeness. How many 'Hail Marys' we have recited in life! Mary does not forget our words: 'pray for us now and at the hour of our death'. And for those who have to bid farewell to loved ones, the Church offers hope when it prays: 'Lord, for your faithful people life is changed, not ended. When the body of our earthly dwelling lies in death we gain an everlasting dwelling place in heaven.'

The Last Things
'Let me go to the house of the Father'

On the evening of Saturday, 2 April 2005, as he lay dying, Pope John Paul indicated that he would like to hear the Gospel of John, a Gospel he particularly loved. It was read out slowly to him, probably by Bishop Stanisław Dziwisz, who had been his faithful secretary since 1966. At a certain point, he managed to whisper words discerned by those present as: 'Let me go to the house of the Father.' These were his last words, an echo of a phrase of the early Church martyr Ignatius of Antioch who, joyfully going to his martyrdom, described hearing the voice of the Spirit within him, like living 'water' welling up and whispering the invitation: 'Come to the Father.' John Paul II's mission was now at an end. He was passing over into the next life.

How would John Paul have viewed this entrance into heaven, the house of the Father? Of course, that moment is so uniquely personal that no one can say. Nevertheless, from his writings and interviews we do know his thoughts on what are often called the 'Last Things' – death, judgment, heaven, hell, and purgatory. For instance, in an interview with Vittorio Messori he recalled how, in the past, sermons were often given on the Last Things, resulting in 'many people ... drawn to conversion and confession.'[212] Such sermons, though not doing justice to all aspects of biblical revelation, went to the heart of people's inner world, stirred their conscience and had a profound saving effect on them.

Perhaps in recalling the contents of those homilies, he is also allowing us see something of how he approached his own definitive encounter in death with the One he had loved his whole life long:

> Remember that at the end you will present yourself before
> God with your entire life. Before his judgment seat you
> will be responsible for all of your actions, you will be
> judged not only on your actions and on your words but
> also on your thoughts, even the most secret.[213]

It wouldn't be fair, however, to limit John Paul's thoughts on death simply to these points. He went well beyond a concern for his individual soul. Among the many treasures he had taken away from the Second Vatican Council was an expanded notion of what salvation means. For instance, the document on the Church, *Lumen Gentium*, presents us with a vast canvas displaying the renewal of all things in Christ. The whole human race, together with the entire world, will be perfectly renewed in Christ. The works we do on earth and our relationships, if lived in love, will be part – in a transformed way – of the new heavens and new earth.

True to his personalist philosophy, John Paul viewed death as a supreme act. It is an act of obedience, the final choice we make at the end of a life made up of many choices along the way. He knows Matthew's Gospel account of the Last Judgement (Mt 25) and he quotes St John of the Cross, the Spanish mystic who so influenced his thinking: 'At the evening of our life we will be judged on love.' Death is our supreme act of abandoning of ourselves into love. And yet John Paul recognises there will be judgement.

The fact of judgement is also a question of justice. People sense that there must be Someone who, in the end, will be able to speak the truth about the good and evil which humanity does; that terrible crimes will not go unpunished. Admittedly, as John Paul explains, 'a profound mystery surrounds the manner in which justice and mercy meet in God when he judges men and their history'.[214] However, he emphasises above all that there is reason for great hope:

> God, who is the just judge, the Judge who rewards good
> and punishes evil is none other than the God ... of Christ
> who is his Son. This God is, above all, Love. Not just
> Mercy, but Love. Not only the Father of the prodigal son,
> but the Father who 'gives his only Son, so that everyone
> who believes in him might not perish but might have
> eternal life' (cf. Jn 3:16).[215]

Heaven, John Paul wrote, is 'the fullness of the good that the human heart desires beyond the limits of all that can be our lot in this earthly life. It is the maximum fullness of God's goodness towards us'.[216] In heaven we will participate in Christ's resurrection. In Christ we will share forever in the life of mutual love of the Trinity. Already through faith we anticipate that life of heaven. But in heaven there will be the fulfilment of the world, a cosmic consummation, a gathering of peoples, 'a new heaven and a new earth'.

The issue of hell is one that has disturbed great thinkers in the Church. The doctrine refers to a definitive choice that we can make to separate ourselves and to remain isolated from God and in total lack of communion with anyone. That is hell. John Paul recognises that many ask: how can a loving God permit us to reject him definitively? Yet it was out of respect for the great gift of our human freedom that the Church rejected the theory that everyone would definitely be saved after death. After all, love of God and neighbour cannot be forced. But can we say that anyone is definitely in hell? The Church has never made any pronouncement about this. As John Paul states, 'Even when Jesus says of Judas, the traitor, "It would be better for that man if he had never been born" (Mt 26:24), his words do not allude for certain to eternal damnation.'[217]

Regarding purgatory, John Paul found the writings of John of the Cross helpful. He saw purgatory as a spiritual preparation for entrance into the perfection of love that is eternal union with the living God. John of the Cross wrote of the 'living flame of love': God makes us pass through an interior purgatory of our sensual and spiritual nature so that we are ready to enter the perfection of love.

Passing over to the next life, then, for John Paul II would have been understood as an event of love: 'Here we do not find ourselves before a mere tribunal. We present ourselves before the power of Love itself. Above all else, it is Love that judges. God, who is Love judges through love.'[218]

John Paul's words, 'Let me go to the house of the Father,' indicate a lot. He saw himself entering definitively into the bosom of the Father. He believed in life beyond death and affirmed: 'I believe in the resurrection of the body', 'I believe in the forgiveness of sins and in life everlasting.' At his Funeral Mass, Cardinal Ratzinger, referring to John Paul II's practice of coming to the window of the Apostolic Palace to give his blessing *Urbi et Orbi* (to the city of Rome and to the world), concluded that 'we can be sure that our beloved Pope is standing today at the window of the Father's house, that he sees us and blesses us'.[219]

The Saints and Martyrs
'They proved that love is stronger than death'

We can only imagine that there must have been quite a celebration when John Paul reached the gates of heaven. After all, it has often been said of him that he was a 'maker of saints'. In his almost twenty-seven years as Pope he canonised 482 saints – more than the Church had in the four hundred years since Pope Sixtus V provided the official criterion for the recognition of sanctity in 1588. Including those he beatified the number rises to 1338.

How can we explain this phenomenon in Pope John Paul's papacy? On the one hand, there's a simple technical reason – he sped up the procedures necessary for the Church to declare a person a saint. However, there's more to it than that. The Second Vatican Council powerfully underlined the universal call to holiness – it was one of the great themes rediscovered there. In the New Testament, for instance, we hear St Paul using the term 'saints' when referring simply to Christians. In other words, holiness is not the reserve of the elite few in convents or monasteries. It is a calling that all baptised people receive: you've been given a great gift of a new life in baptism, now become what you are, be a saint together with your sister and brother Christians.

But what is holiness? The definition given by Vatican II is: 'the perfection of love'. This is a wonderful summary statement and something we can all strive for, regardless of our occupation, age or social condition. It doesn't mean perfectionism, or this or that particular practice or penance, but rather following the way of love that God has marked out for each one of us. As John of the Cross put it, 'where there is no love, put love and there you will find love'. The Beatitudes can be lived by anyone in any context.

Recently I heard someone comment on discovering that somebody they knew was being considered for beatification, 'But she was just an ordinary person like me.' Indeed, that is the whole point! As Augustine realised in the fourth century: 'if they can, why not me too?'

John Paul canonised 258 lay saints, including Frédérick Ozanam, professor at the Sarbonne and founder of the St Vincent de Paul society, and Gianna Beretta Molla, who died giving birth to her daughter. And he was particularly pleased to beatify Luigi Beltrame Quattrocchi and Maria Corsini, the first husband and wife to be canonised. There were many popular saints among those canonised or beatified by the Polish Pope – such as Mother Teresa of Calcutta and Padre Pio – but so many other names could also be listed in the roll call: Mother Théodore Guérin, Katharine Drexel, Damien of Molokai, Edmund Rice and the Irish Martyrs, Columba Marmion, Josemaría Escriva, Mary Helen MacKillop, Josephine Bakhita. The list is enormous. Pope John Paul also dedicated an encyclical letter, *Slavorum Apostoli*, to saints Cyril and Methodius.[220]

The martyrs were a special category of saints that John Paul highlighted. Many of them had suffered under the totalitarian regimes of the twentieth century, ending up in Gulags, concentration camps and gas chambers. The theme of martyrdom is one that John Paul returned to often. It is sobering to recall that there were probably more martyrs in the twentieth century than in the preceding history of the Church. Consider Maximilian Kolbe, the 'martyr of charity', who, having offered to take the place of a man with a family, was killed in Auschwitz – the concentration camp that John Paul called the 'Calvary of our time', a place of such a terrifying disregard for the human being. Also killed there was Edith Stein, the great academic scholar, student of the famous philosopher Husserl, Jewess convert to Christianity and Carmelite nun, who was canonised by Pope John Paul in 1998.

On 7 May 2000, during the Jubilee Year, he presided over a ceremony that recognised the witness of all Christians during the twentieth century:

> How many Christians in the course of the twentieth century, on every continent, showed their love of Christ by the shedding of blood! They underwent forms of persecution both old and new, they experienced hatred and exclusion, violence and murder. Many countries of ancient Christian tradition once more became lands where fidelity to the Gospel demanded a very high price. In our century 'the witness to Christ borne even to the shedding of blood has become a common inheritance of Catholics, Orthodox, Anglicans and Protestants' ...

> Where hatred seemed to corrupt the whole of life leaving
> no escape from its logic, they proved that 'love is stronger
> than death' ... May the memory of these brothers and
> sisters of ours remain always vivid.[221]

For John Paul the twentieth-century martyrs were at the 'foundation
of a new world, a new Europe and a new civilization'.[222] Along with the
saints, they proved that love is stronger than death.

Epilogue

Pope John Paul II and Pope Benedict XVI
'He placed a great, very cordial, and profound trust in me'

For the best part of twenty-five years, Cardinal Ratzinger met with Pope John Paul II every Friday evening to present him with the work of the Congregation for the Doctrine of the Faith. He also met with the Pope and his collaborators at other times, such as on Tuesdays from 12 p.m. to 3 p.m., and a deep bond developed between them.

The Polish Pope appointed the German Cardinal Prefect of the Congregation for the Doctrine of the Faith on 25 November 1981. He had read Ratzinger's classic book, *Introduction to Christianity*, and it had made an impression on him. From the beginning, as Pope Benedict has recently commented, John Paul II placed 'a great, very cordial, and profound trust in me'. Indeed, if there has been a seamless transition between the pontificates 'it helped that everyone knew that John Paul II liked me. That we had reached a deep spiritual understanding.' Our present Pope sees himself as 'a modest figure who is trying to continue what John Paul II accomplished as a gift'. [223]

In his homily at the funeral of Pope John Paul, Cardinal Ratzinger referred to three sayings of Jesus that he believed summed up how the late Pope saw himself as a priest. The first was: 'You did not choose me, but I chose you. And I appointed you to go and bear fruit, fruit that will last' (Jn 15:16). The second: 'The good shepherd lays down his life for the sheep' (Jn 10:11). And the third: 'As the Father has loved me, so I have loved you; abide in my love' (Jn 15:9). 'In these three sayings,' Ratzinger commented, 'we see the heart and soul of our Holy Father. He really went everywhere, untiringly, in order to bear fruit, fruit that lasts.'
In the course of an interview with Cardinal Ratzinger several years ago, Peter Seewald put it to him that sometimes it was believed that Pope John Paul II would be inconceivable without Cardinal Ratzinger, and Cardinal Ratzinger without the Pope. [224] Seewald told him, 'you are considered the brilliant theologian at the side of a philosopher' and went as far as to claim

that Ratzinger had been 'a chief shaper of [Pope John Paul II's] pontificate. Without this special Wojtyła–Ratzinger connection, the Church would likely have taken a different course at the end of the millennium. In his reply, Ratzinger commented that his role should not be overestimated. Nevertheless, he did admit 'the Pope trusts me; we've always discussed very important doctrinal matters with each other and continue to do so ... But the Pope has very much his own course.'[225]

From this response comes the impression of a warm brotherly exchange of information, mutual correction and appreciation of different viewpoints. This perhaps also explains why Pope John Paul clearly wanted Cardinal Ratzinger in office long after the German's official retirement date. As Ratzinger's seventy-fifth birthday approached (the age bishops normally submit their letter of resignation), Pope John Paul said to him 'You do not have to write the letter at all, for I want to have you to the end.'[226]

Pope Benedict admired the great approval his predecessor met with as a champion for human rights, peace and freedom. He sensed the Polish Pope was called to guide the Church at a particularly intense moment of its history:

> Karol Wojtyła was sent by God to the Church ... in a very
> specific, critical situation, in which, on the one hand,
> the Marxist generation, the 1968 generation, called the
> entire West into question and in which, conversely, real
> Socialism feel to pieces. In the midst of this conflict to
> open a path for a breakthrough to faith and to show that it
> is the centre and the way – that was a historic moment of a
> special sort.[227]

It would be easy to imagine that Benedict might have faced a personal challenge in following such a hugely significant papacy, not least since his predecessor was regarded as something like a celebrity. John Paul II's sheer physical presence, his voice and gestures produced a media sensation and had a powerful effect on people. Pope Benedict might not have the same reputation or the same voice, but with the meek confidence of faith he tells us how he overcame that challenge:

> I simply told myself that I am who I am. I don't try to be
> someone else. What I can give I give, and what I can't give

I don't try to give, either. I don't try to make myself into
something I am not.[228]

During a Polish television programme, aired on 16 October 2005, the
anniversary of Pope John Paul II's election in 1978, Benedict remarked:

> I consider it my essential and personal mission not so
> much to produce many new documents but to see to it
> that [John Paul II's documents] are assimilated, because
> they are a very rich treasure, the authentic interpretation
> of Vatican II.[229]

In an observation that is also perhaps autobiographical, Pope Benedict
underlines the value of suffering in Pope John Paul's pontificate:

> I think it was very important for the Church herself to
> receive this lesson in suffering after a great burst of activity
> and to see that the Church can also be governed through
> suffering and that it is precisely through suffering that she
> grows to maturity and is enlivened.[230]

For John Paul II, by looking to the Crucified, Forsaken and Risen
Christ, suffering can be transformed into love. And this is how the
Church goes ahead. This was, perhaps, the final silent but deepest
'teaching' of his life and ministry – one that clearly struck and remains
with Pope Benedict XVI, whose very first encyclical bears the title *Deus
Caritas Est – God is Love.*

.

Notes

1. John Paul II, *Memory and Identity: Personal Reflections*, London: Weidenfeld & Nicolson, 2005, p. 187.
2. John Paul II, *Gift and Mystery: On the Fiftieth Anniversary of My Priestly Ordination*, London: CTS, 1997, p. 6. All further references in this chapter are taken from *Gift and Mystery* and page numbers are given in the text.
3. John Paul II, *Gift and Mystery*, pp. 50–1.
4. As Pope he issued an apostolic letter on John of the Cross, *Teacher of Faith* (14 December 1990). See also his address during a visit to Sevogia on 5 November 1982.
5. See I. Colosio, 'Il P. Maestro Reginaldo Garrigou-Lagrange', *Vita Cristiana* 34 (1965), p. 61, quoted in Jesús Castellano Cervera, 'La rilettura della fede in Giovanni della Croce (1948) e il magistero odierno di Giovanni Paolo II. Continuità e novità', in Giuseppe Marco Salvati and Alberto Lo Presti, eds., *Karol Wojtyła un papa venuto dall'Angelicum*, Rome: Città Nuova, 2009, pp. 115–31, p. 121.
6. Quoted in Tad Szulc, *Pope John Paul II: The Biography*, New York and London: Scribner, 1995, p. 152.
7. See John M. McDermott, ed., *The Thought of Pope John Paul II*, Rome: PUG, 1993.
8. Karol Wojtyła, *Person and Community: Selected Essays*, tr. Theresa Sandok, New York: Peter Lang, 1993, p. 38.
9. John Paul II, *Gift and Mystery*, pp. 93–4.
10. Ibid., p. 64.
11. See Pope John Paul's comment in his interview with André Frossard, *Be Not Afraid! John Paul II Speaks Out on His Life, His Beliefs and His Inspiring Vision for Humanity*, New York: St Martin's Press, 1984, p. 110.
12. John Paul II, 'Encyclical Letter on the Redeemer of Humanity', *Redemptor Hominis* (3 April 1979), 14.
13. Ibid., 13.
14. Second Vatican Council, 'Constitution on the Church in the Modern World', *Gaudium et Spes* (7 December 1965), 22. The word 'man' in the text has an inclusive sense.
15. *Gaudium et Spes*, 1 and 22 respectively.
16. George Weigel, *Witness to Hope: The Biography of Pope John Paul II*, London: HarperCollins, 1999, p. 160ff. See also Michael Walsh, *John Paul II: A Biography*, London: HarperCollins, 1995, p. 27ff.
17. Karol Wojtyła, *Collected Poems*, tr. Jerzy Peterkiewicz, London: Hutchinson, 1982, p. 116.

18. See Karol Wojtyła, *Sources of Renewal: The Implementation of the Second Vatican Council*, London: Collins Fount, 1980.

19. From a note written by Pope John Paul II during the spiritual exercises in the Jubilee Year 2000 (12–18 March) and inserted into his Last Will and Testament.

20. George Weigel, *The End and the Beginning: Pope John Paul II – The Victory of Freedom, the Last Years, the Legacy*, New York: Doubleday, 2010.

21. See Tad Szulc, *John Paul II: The Biography*, pp. 242–5.

22. Quoted by Mariusz Frukacz, editor of the Catholic weekly magazine, *Niedziela*, during an interview with Antonio Gaspari in *Zenit* on 17 February 2011.

23. Quoted in Tad Szulc, p. 247.

24. George Weigel, *Witness to Hope*, p. 232.

25. John Paul II, *Memory and Identity*, p. 50.

26. John Paul II, *Crossing the Threshold of Hope*, London: Jonathan Cape, 1994, p. 199.

27. Homily for the Inauguration of the Pontificate of John Paul II, St Peter's Square (22 October 1978).

28. See *Redemptor Hominis*, 1 and the 'Encyclical Letter on Certain Fundamental Questions of the Church's Moral Teaching', *Veritatis Splendor* (6 August 1993), 2.

29. *Redemptor Hominis*, 1.

30. *Gaudium et Spes*, 24.

31. *Veritatis Splendor*, 20.

32. *Redemptor Hominis*, 14.

33. *Gaudium et Spes*, 22.

34. John Paul II, *Memory and Identity*, p. 6.

35. John Paul II, 'Encyclical Letter on Divine Mercy', *Dives in Misericordia* (30 November 1980), 53.

36. John Paul II, 'Apostolic Letter on the Dignity and Vocation of Women on the Occasion of the Marian Year', *Mulieris Dignitatem* (15 August 1988), 8.

37. *Dives in Misericordia*, 7. All further references in this chapter are taken from *Dives in Misericordia* and numbers are given in the text.

38. Quoted in Remo Piccolomini and Natalino Monopoli, *Vita di Papa Giovanni Paolo II*, Padua: Messaggero, 2008, p. 20.

39. John Paul II, 'Encyclical Letter the Holy Spirit in the Life of the Church and the World', *Dominum et Vivificantem* (18 May 1986), 31.

40. Second Vatican Council, 'Constitution on the Nature of the Church', *Lumen Gentium* (21 November 1964), 1. See also Piero Coda, 'The Ecclesial Movements, Gift of the Spirit', in The Pontifical Council for the Laity, *Movements in the Church*, Vatican City, 1999, pp. 78–80.

41. See *Dominum et Vivificantem*, 63.
42. Ibid., 66.
43. John Paul II, 'Encyclical Letter on the Permanent Validity of the Church's Missionary Mandate', *Redemptoris Missio* (12 July 1990), 29.
44. *Redemptoris Missio*, 29, from an address to the Cardinals and the Roman Curia (22 December 1986).
45. *Redemptor Hominis*, 18.
46. John Paul II, 'Christmas Address to the Roman Curia' (22 December 1986). See also the English edition of *L'Osservatore Romano*, 5 January 1987, pp. 6–7. Unless otherwise stated, all further references in this chapter are taken from the 1986 Christmas Address. Reproduced in Francesco Gioia, ed., *Interreligious Dialogue*, Boston: Pauline Books & Media, 1997, pp. 359–66.
47. *Gaudium et Spes*, 22.
48. *Lumen Gentium*, 13.
49. See John McNerney, *Footbridge Towards the Other: An Introduction to the Philosophy and Poetry of John Paul II*, London: T&T Clark, 2003.
50. Henri de Lubac, *At the Service of the Gospel*, San Francisco: Ignatius, 1993, pp. 171–2.
51. Maciej Zięba, *The Surprising Pope: Understanding the Thought of John Paul II*, tr. Karolina Weening, New York: Lexington Books, 2000, p. 24.
52. *Veritatis Splendor*, 40.
53. Cardinal Joseph Ratzinger, 'Le 14 encicliche' in *Il Regno-documenti* 19 (2003), pp. 586–9, p. 589.
54. John Paul II, 'Encyclical Letter on the Relationship between Faith and Reason', *Fides et Ratio* (15 September 1998), 17.
55. See Cardinal Joseph Ratzinger, 'Le 14 encicliche', p. 589.
56. *Fides et Ratio*, 1.
57. Avery Dulles, 'Mary at the Dawn of the New Millennium', *America* 178 (1998/3), pp. 8–19, p. 9. For an expanded treatment of material in this chapter see Brendan Leahy, 'Totus Tuus: The Mariology of John Paul II' in William Oddie, ed., *John Paul the Great: Maker of the Post-Conciliar Church*, London: CTS, 2003, pp. 69–94.
58. See M. Malinski, *Pope John Paul II*, London: Burns & Oates, 1979, pp. 28–35; George Weigel, *Witness to Hope*, pp. 60–2.
59. André Frossard, *Be Not Afraid!*, p. 125.
60. Stefano De Fiores, *Maria nella Teologia Contemporanea*, Rome: Centro Mariano Monfortano, 1991, pp. 657–8.
61. John Paul II, 'Encyclical Letter on Blessed Virgin Mary in the Life of the Pilgrim Church', *Redemptoris Mater* (25 March 1987), 18. All further references in this chapter are taken from *Redemptoris Mater* and numbers are given in the text.

62. See John Paul II, *Memory and Identity*, p. 179.
63. *Dives in Misericordia*, 7.
64. Ibid., 13.
65. Ibid., 14.
66. John Paul II, *Memory and Identity*, p. 187.
67. Karol Wojtyła, *Sign of Contradiction*, tr. Mary Smith, Middlegreen, Slough: St Paul Publications, 1979, pp. 99–100.
68. This followed on from the 'Encyclical Letter on the Eucharist in its Relationship to the Church', *Ecclesia de Eucharistia* (17 April 2003).
69. John Paul II, 'Apostolic Letter for the Year of the Eucharist', *Mane Nobiscum Domine* (October 2004), 1. All further references in this chapter are taken from *Mane Nobiscum Domine* and numbers are given in the text.
70. John Paul II, 'Apostolic Letter on the Church at the Beginning of the New Millennium', *Novo Millennio Ineunte* (6 January 2001), 43.
71. Ibid. See also Thomas Norris, *The Trinity: Life of God, Hope for Humanity*, New York: New City, 2009.
72. *Novo Millenio Ineunte*, 43. All further references in this chapter are taken from *Novo Millenio Ineunte* and numbers are given in the text.
73. John Paul II, *Crossing the Threshold of Hope*, p. 19.
74. John Paul II, 'Encyclical Letter on the Holy Spirit in the Life of the Church and the World', *Dominum et Vivificantem* (18 May 1986), 65.
75. John Paul II, *Crossing the Threshold of Hope*, pp. 17–18.
76. Ibid., p. 18.
77. Ibid., p. 23.
78. See Cardinal Martins' comments made during an iterview with H2O News (7 March 2011).
79. John Paul II, 'Apostolic Letter on the Christian Meaning of Human Suffering', *Salvifici Doloris* (11 February 1984), 11.
80. *Novo Millennio Ineunte*, 25.
81. *Salvifici Doloris*, 18. Unless otherwise stated, all further references in this chapter are taken from *Salvifici Doloris* and numbers are given in the text.
82. John Paul II, Angelus Message (29 May 1994).
83. *Novo Millennio Ineunte*, 29. For an expanded treatment of the material in this chapter, see Brendan Leahy, 'Living the Rosary', *Furrow* 54 (2003), pp. 282–6.
84. John Paul II, 'Apostolic Letter on the Rosary', *Rosarium Virginis Mariae* (16 October 2002), 26.
85. Rowan Williams, *Ponder These Things: Praying with Icons of the Virgin*, Norwich: Canterbury Press, 2002, p. 62ff.
86. See also *Novo Millennio Ineunte*, 33.

87. *Rosarium Virginis Mariae*, 25.
88. Avery Dulles, *The Splendor of Faith: The Theological Vision of Pope John Paul II*, New York: Crossroad, 1999, p. 46.
89. John Paul II, 'Apostolic Letter on the Laity in the Church and the World, *Christifideles Laici* (30 December 1988), 20.
90. *Lumen Gentium*, 4.
91. *Novo Millennio Ineunte*, 29.
92. Klaus Hemmerle, *Brücken zum Credo*, Freiburg: Herder, 1984, p. 20.
93. John Paul II to the Roman Curia, *L'Osservatore Romano* [English edition], 11 January 1988, pp. 6–8.
94. See John Paul II's 'Address to the EEC' (20 May 1985).
95. John Paul II, 'The Crisis of European Culture' in *L'Osservatore Romano* [English edition], 13 December 1982, pp. 6–7.
96. John Paul II, Homily given during a celebration of the word in honour of St John of the Cross at Segovia, *L'Osservatore Romano* [Italian edition], (4 November 1982).
97. See also Brendan Leahy, 'The Triune God's Reply to Europe's Contemporary Cry', in Liam Bergin, ed., *According to Your Word*, Dublin: Four Courts Press, 2007, pp. 47–60.
98. John Paul II, Address to the Cardinals of the United States (23 April 2002). Unless otherwise stated, all further references in this chapter are taken from the 2002 Address to the Cardinals.
99. George Weigel, *The End and the Beginning*, pp. 418–19.
100. George Weigel, 'The Soul of John Paul II', Lecture delivered at Oxford (6 March, 2001).
101. John Paul II, *Gift and Mystery*, p. 24.
102. John Paul II, 'Apostolic Exhortation on the Vocation and the Mission of the Lay Faithful in the Church and in the World', *Christifideles Laici* (30 December 1988), 55.
103. George Weigel, *Witness to Hope*, p. 658.
104. John Paul II, *Gift and Mystery*, p. 72.
105. John Paul II, 'Apostolic Exhortation on the Formation of Priests for the Circumstances of the Present Day', *Pastores Dabo Vobis* (25 March 1992), 15.
106. Ibid., 12.
107. John Paul II, *Gift and Mystery*, p. 88.
108. John Paul II, 'Apostolic Exhortation on the Consecrated Life and its Mission in the Church and in the World', *Vita Consecreta* (25 March 1996), 3. All further references in this chapter are taken from *Vita Consecreta* and numbers are given in the text.
109. Pope John Paul II to CELAM meeting in Port-au-Prince, Haiti (9 March 1983).

110. *Novo Millennio Ineunte*, 40.
111. John Paul II, 'Apostolic Letter to those Responsible for Communications', *The Rapid Development* (24 January 2005), 14.
112. Ibid., 3.
113. *Novo Millennio Ineunte*, 16.
114. Ibid., 56.
115. John Paul II, 'Message to the World Congress of Ecclesial Movements and New Communities' (27–29 May 1998), 2.
116. Cardinal Stanislaw Ryłko, Preface to 'Pontifical Council for the Laity', *The Beauty of Being Christian*, Vatican, 2007, p. xii.
117. John Paul II, 'Meeting with Ecclesial Movements and New Communities' (30 May 1998), 4. All further references in this chapter are taken from 'Meeting with Ecclesial Movements and New Communities' and numbers are given in the text.
118. *Economist*, 25 March 2000, p. 47.
119. John Paul II, 'Message for the 90th World Day of Migrants and Refugees 2004: Migration with a View to Peace' (15 December 2003), 5.
120. John Paul II, 'Message for the Celebration of the World Day of Peace 1986: Peace is a Value with No Frontiers North-South, East-West: Only One Peace' (1 January 1986), 4. Printed in Brendan Leahy, ed., *No Peace Without Justice, No Justice Without Forgiveness: Messages for Peace from Pope John Paul II*, Dublin: Veritas, 2005, pp. 108–119, p. 113ff. See also Kevin Doran, *Solidarity: A Synthesis of Personalism and Communalism in the Thought of Karol Wojtyła/Pope John Paul II*, New York: Peter Lang, 1996.
121. Ibid.
122. John Paul II, 'Vespers Liturgy on the Occasion of the 40th Anniversary of the Promulgation of the Conciliar Decree *Unitatis Redintegratio*', Homily (13 November 2004), 4.
123. John Paul II, *Crossing the Threshold of Hope*, pp. 152–4.
124. John Paul II, 'Encyclical Letter on Commitment to Ecumenism', *Ut Unum Sint* (25 May 1995), 9.
125. John Paul II, 'Address to the Secretariat for Christian Unity' (8 February 1980).
126. Ibid.
127. Quoted in Kevin J.P. McDonald, 'The Legacy of Pope John Paul II: Ecumenical Dialogue', in Michael Hayes and Gerald O'Collins, *The Legacy of John Paul*, op. cit., pp. 110–1.
128. John Paul II, Homily at the Ecumenical Commemoration of the Wtinesses to the Faith in the Twentieth Century (7 May 2000).
129. *Redemptoris Missio*, 57.

130. John Paul II, 'To Representatives of Various Religions of India' (Madras, 5 February 1986). Reproduced in Francesco Gioia (ed.), *Interreligious Dialogue*, pp. 324–7, p. 326.

131. John Paul II, 'Address to the Jewish Community of Rome', Synagogue of Rome (13 April 1986).

132. Quoted in Garry O'Connor, *Universal Father: A Life of Pope John Paul II*, London: Bloomsbury, 2005, p. 35.

133. John Paul II, 'Meeting with Representatives of Roman Jewish Organisations' (12 March 1979).

134. Jack Bemporad quoted in *The Jewish Standard* (21 September 2006).

135. John Paul II, Address at the meeting with Muslim leaders at Umayyad Great Mosque, Damascus (6 May 2001).

136. John Paul II, Message on the Occasion of Eid-al-Fitr, 1991. Quoted in Francesco Gioia, *Interreligious Dialogue*, pp. 451–3, p. 453.

137. John Paul II, *Gift and Mystery*, pp. 94–5.

138. John Paul II, 'Address to the Pontifical Academy of Sciences on the Occasion of the Centenary of the Birth of Albert Einstein' (10 November 1979).

139. John Paul II, 'Address to the Pontifical Academy of the Sciences' (23 October 1996).

140. Letter of Pope John Paul II to George V. Coyne S.J., Director of the Vatican Observatory (1 June 1988).

141. Ibid.

142. Stephen Jay Gould, *Rocks of Ages: Science and Religion in the Fullness of Life*, London: Jonathan Cape, 2001, p. 82.

143. John Paul II, *Gift and Mystery*, pp. 61–2.

144. See *Christifideles Laici*, 26.

145. John Paul II, 'Address to the Clergy of Rome' (9 November 1978).

146. John Paul II, 'Address to the Parish Movement', Paul VI Hall (3 May 1986).

147. Ibid.

148. Quoted in Tad Szulc, *Pope John Paul II: The Biography*, pp. 160–1.

149. John Paul II, *Letter to Families* (2 February 1994), 2.

150. Ibid.

151. 'The Second Vatican Council Decree on the Laity', *Apostolicam Actuositatem* (18 November 1965), 11; *Lumen Gentium*, 11; 'Apostolic Letter on the Family', *Familiaris Consortio* (22 November 1981), 21.

152. *Familiaris Consortio*, 84.

153. John Paul II, *Letter to Children in the Year of the Family* (13 December 1994), 1. All further references in this chapter are taken from the *Letter to Children*, 1.

154. John Paul II, *Crossing the Threshold of Hope*, p. 125.

155. Ibid, p. 124.
156. Ibid., p. 125.
157. John Paul II, 'Apostolic Letter to the Youth of the World on the Occasion of International Youth Year', *Delecti Amici* (31 March 1985), 3.
158. Ibid., 4.
159. Ibid., 7.
160. See Father Lombardi's reflection on Vatican Television's *Octava Dies*, quoted in *Zenit* (14 January 2011).
161. John Paul II, 'Message for the Fifth World Day of the Sick' (11 February 1997), 4. See also *Salvifici Doloris*, 31.
162. John Paul II, weekly catechesis on the 'theology of the body' (16 January 1980). For an English translation see John Paul II, *The Theology of the Body: Human Love in the Divine Plan*, Boston: Pauline Books and Media, 1997.
163. See John F. Crosby, 'John Paul II's Vision of Sexuality and Marriage: The Mystery of "Fair Love"', Geoffrey Gneuhs, ed., *The Legacy of Pope John Paul II: His Contribution to Catholic Thought*, New York: Crossroad, 2000, pp. 52–70.
164. Quoted in Garry O'Connor, *Universal Father*, p. 134.
165. John Paul II, 'Apostolic Letter on the Preparation for the Jubilee Year 2000', *Tertio Millennio Adveniente* (12 November 1994), 10.
166. John Paul II, *Memory and Identity*, pp. 91–2.
167. John Paul II, 'Address to UNESCO, June 1980', quoted in *L'Osservatore Romano* [English edition], 23 June 1980, pp. 9–12.
168. John Paul II, *Memory and Identity*, p. 89.
169. John Paul II, 'Homily during the Rite of the Possession of the Chair of the Bishop of Rome', Basilica of St John Lateran (12 November 1978).
170. *Fides et Ratio*, 71.
171. Ibid., 1.
172. Ibid., 2.
173. See Brendan Purcell, '*Fides et Ratio*: Charter for the Third Millennium' in James McEvoy, ed., *The Challenge of Truth: Reflections on Fides et Ratio*, Dublin: Veritas, 2002, pp. 240–253.
174. John Paul II, 'Address to the Diplomatic Corps' (13 January 2003), n. 4.
175. Cardinal Sodano, 'Al Servizio della Pace', *Regno-documenti* (2003/19), p. 593.
176. John Paul II, 'Homily at the Mass in Drogheda, Ireland' (29 September 1979), 11.
177. John Paul II, 'Message for the Celebration of the World Day of Peace' (1 January 1986), 7.
178. See Luigi Accattoli, *When a Pope Asks Forgiveness: The Mea Culpas of John Paul II*, New York: Alba House, 1998.

179. *Karol: The Man Who Became Pope* (2005), directed by Giacomo Battiato and produced by Pietro Valsecchi. Starring Polish actor Piotr Adamczyk as Karol Wojtyła.
180. John Paul II, *Memory and Identity*, pp. 15–17.
181. John Paul II, 'Message for the Celebration of the World Day of Peace', (1 January 2002), 3.
182. *Dives in Misericordia*, 4.
183. International Theological Commission, *Memory and Reconcilliation: The Church and the Faults of the Past*, December 1999.
184. John Paul II, 'Confession of Sins and Asking for Forgiveness', Universal Prayer (March 2000).
185. John Paul II, *Gift and Mystery*, pp. 21–2.
186. John Paul II, 'Encyclical Letter on Human Work', *Laborem Exercens* (14 September 1981), 1. All further references in this chapter are taken from *Laborem Excercens* and numbers are given in the text.
187. See Tad Szulc, *Pope John Paul II: The Biography*, p. 108.
188. Ibid., p. 107.
189. On the notion of 'structures of sin' see John Paul II, *Sollicitudo Rei Socialis* (30 December 1987), 36–40.
190. John Paul II, 'Encyclical Letter on the Hundredth Anniversary of *Rerum Novarum*', *Centesimus Annus* (1 May, 1991), 52.
191. John Paul II, 'Message for the Celebration of the World Day of Peace' (1 January 2000), 14.
192. John Paul II, *Compendium of the Social Doctrine of the Church*, Libreria Editrice Vaticana, 2005 (reprint), p. 564.
193. John Paul II, 'Encyclical Letter on the Value and Invoilability of Human Life', *Evangelium Vitae* (25 March 1995), 1.
194. Quoted in George Weigel, *Witness to Hope*, p. 759.
195. *Evangelium Vitae*, 4.
196. Ibid., 21.
197. *Gaudium et Spes*, 36.
198. Ibid., 27.
199. See *Mulieris Dignitatem*, 14.
200. *Evangelium Vitae*, 73. All further references in this chapter are taken from *Evangelium Vitae* and numbers are given in the text.
201. See also *Christifideles Laici*, especially 49.
202. *Mulieris Dignitatem*, 15.
203. John Paul II, *Letter to Women* (29 June 1995), 3. Unless otherwise stated, all further references in this chapter are taken from the *Letter to Women* and numbers are given in the text.
204. John Paul II, Angelus Message (16 July 1995).

205. John Paul II, Angelus Message (14 August 1995).
206. John Paul II, 'Apostolic Letter on Reserving Priestly Ordination to Men Alone', *Ordinatio Sacerdotalis* (22 May 1994), 4.
207. *Vita Consecrata*, 58.
208. John Paul II, *Letter to Artists* (4 April 1999), 1. Unless otherwise stated, all further references in this chapter are taken from the *Letter to Artists* and numbers are given in the text.
209. See Karol Wojtyła, *The Collected Plays and Writings on Theater*, tr. Boleslaw Taborski, Berkeley: University of California Press, 1987, p. 379.
210. John Paul II, *Letter to the Elderly* (1 October 1999), 1. Unless otherwise stated, all further references in this chapter are taken from the *Letter to the Elderly* and numbers are given in the text.
211. For a collection of writings from his final year in this world, see John Paul II, *Silence Transformed into Life*, New York: New City, 2006.
212. John Paul II, *Crossing the Threshold of Hope*, pp. 178–187.
213. Ibid., p. 179.
214. John Paul II, *Memory and Identity*, p. 152.
215. John Paul II, *Crossing the Threshold of Hope*, p. 184.
216. John Paul II, General Audience (21 April 1982).
217. John Paul II, Crossing the *Threshold of Hope*, p. 186
218. Ibid., p. 187.
219. Cardinal Ratzinger, 'Homily for the Funeral Mass of Pope John Paul II' (8 April 2005).
220. John Paul II, 'Encyclical Letter Commemorating the Eleventh Centenary of the Evangelizing Work of Saints Cyril and Methodius', *Slavorum Apostoli* (2 June 1985).
221. John Paul II, 'Ecumenical Commemoration of the Witnesses to the Faith in the Twentieth Century' (7 May 2000), 2–4.
222. John Paul II, *Crossing the Threshold of Hope*, p. 177.
223. Benedict XVI, *Light of the World: The Pope, the Church and the Signs of the Times*, San Francisco: Ignatius Press, 2010, p. 19.
224. Joseph Cardinal Ratzinger, *Salt of the Earth: The Church at the End of the Millennium*, San Francisco: Ignatius Press, 1997, pp. 105–6.
225. Ibid.
226. Benedict XVI, *Light of the World*, p. 4.
227. Ibid., p. 66.
228. Ibid.,. p. 112.
229. Quoted in the Preface to Michael Hayes and Gerald O'Collins, *The Legacy of John Paul II*, op. cit. See also William Oddie, ed., *John Paul the Great: Maker of the Post-Conciliar Church*, London: CTS, 2003.
230. Benedict XVI, *Light of the World*, p. 80.

Believe in Love
The Life Ministry and Teachings of John Paul II

Rev. Brendan Leahy is Professor of Systematic Theology at the Pontifical University of St Patrick's College, Maynooth. He is a von Balthasar scholar and ecumenist, and has published books and articles on topics such as John Paul II, the Marian profile of the Church, issues facing the Church in the twenty-first century, the ecclesial movements of the Church, interreligious dialogue and the priesthood.